Canoeist's

Scenarios for Seriou

by

Cliff Jacobson

Illustrations by Cliff Moen

You decide the outcome to twenty-five true
and often life-threatening scenarios—and
get in-depth answers to the most frequently
asked canoeing questions!

ICS Books, Inc.
Merrillville, Indiana

Published by: Cover photo: Photodisc
ICS BOOKS, Inc.
1370 East 86th Place
Merrillville, Indiana 46410
(800) 541-7323

Published in the U.S.A.

All ICS BOOKS titles are printed on 50% recycled paper from pre-
consumer waste. All sheets are processed without using acid.

This text of this book is set in Caslon 224. Design by Matt Gaylen.

Library of Congress Cataloging-in-Publication Data

Jacobson, Cliff
    Canoeist's Q&A: scenarios for serious canoeists /
    by Cliff Jacobson
        p.cm.
    ISBN 1-57034-055-2 (pbk.)
    1. Canoes and canoeing– Miscellanea.#I. Title II. Title:
GV783.J283   1997
797.1'22'02-DC21   96-51756
                                           CIP

Scenarios for Serious Canoeist

Preface

One of the perks of being an outdoors writer is all the wonderful people I get to meet. Hardly a week goes by that I don't get a call or letter from someone who loves wild places and the magic of canoes. Most of the calls are about equipment (which canoe is best, what tent should I buy, etc.) and wilderness trip logistics (I'm doing the Missinaibi River next summer and...), but some address important safety issues and social concerns. The more I canoe, the more I realize that there is much more to canoeing than could be written in a dozen books or told in a month of seminars. In the preface to my first book, Wilderness Canoeing & Camping (1977), I said that, "If you take canoeing seriously (or plan to), you should read every canoe book in print—not once, but many times. Only after you have studied the works of others—and paddled many miles—will you know what's best for you."

I believe that, more so than ever.

Canoeing—especially whitewater and wilderness canoeing—is an experiential sport. One learns by doing and by watching others who know what they're doing. Granted, there are some very good canoeists who have never read a canoeing book or attended a paddling class or outdoor seminar. They've taken their hard knocks, learned from their mistakes and rightfully earned their "expert" status. But the climb to the top wasn't easy. Press these people hard and they'll admit that some well directed homework would probably have smoothed the way.

Canoeists' Q&A is not a HOW TO book on canoeing or camping. Nothing in these pages will tell you how to paddle, where to paddle or why to paddle. And with rare exceptions, it won't suggest what equipment you should bring or leave at home. Instead, it deeply probes the concerns that are part of every canoe trip—from quiet local streams to the Boundary Waters and the Barrens.

There are three parts to this book: SCENARIOS, FAQ's and SHORT FAQ's.

FAQ's are in-depth answers to Frequently Asked Questions. I've interspersed them among lengthy scenarios for variety and a lighter touch.

Short FAQ's provide quick, easy-to-digest solutions to fifteen of the most common canoeing concerns. They're in a special section at the back of the book so you can find them fast.

Scenarios detail serious events that occurred on past canoe trips. Some describe life-threatening situations; others portray inefficient canoeing and camping practices or philosophical or health concerns. All pose a problem which you must solve. Carefully read each scenario then decide what to do. The solutions aren't obvious, and often, there is more than one right answer. Sometimes, there are none at all! There's a list of canoeing words in the back of the book to help you with unfamiliar terms.

Give each problem your best shot then read the ANSWER: BEST PROBABLE ACTION TAKEN scene which tells WHAT HAPPENED. Then, see the following PROBABLE BEST COURSE OF ACTION, which suggests a reasonable plan. My hope is that you'll discuss the scenarios with your friends as you plan your next canoe trip.

Have fun discussing options as you try to beat the experts which, you'll note, don't always make the right decisions. Be aware that no one has a monopoly on good ideas, and that level-headed thinking is the best way to ensure a safe canoeing experience.

If you have questions or scenarios you'd like to share, please write me, care of my publisher. I promise a fast and courteous response. Like I said, no one has a monopoly on good ideas. I'll be proud to learn from yours.

—Cliff Jacobson

Dedication

To Clarissa and Peggy, my wonderful, talented daughters. They follow
their dreams and give steadfast support to mine. No father could be
more proud.

1. In Search Of Big Fish

Scenario

You are canoeing the Fond du Lac River in Northern Saskatche-wan—a remote challenging route that has many rapids and falls which require attention. The weather is good and you are right on schedule. Everyone in the crew is an experienced whitewater paddler.

You have observed that one canoe team frequently lags behind to fish. However, they are strong paddlers and always catch up with the group in an hour or so. Each canoe team has a map and compass, and all major rapids are marked on the map.

The Question

You're the trip leader: should you allow the fishermen to go at their own pace, or require them to stay with the group?

Action Taken

The trip leader allowed the fishermen to go at their own pace, and the group became widely separated. When the forward party reached Thompson Rapids—an approximate eight-foot ledge that spans most of the 100 yard wide river, they decided to portage on the outside of a large sweeping bend. Someone tied a red cowboy handkerchief on a jutting limb to mark the start of the carry.

A recent burn and accompanying thick vegetation forced the portagers away from the river. They were deep in the forest, out of ear-shot, when the fishermen arrived on the scene. Uncertain of the whereabouts of the portage—and unable to see the red cotton marker—the late comers chose to check out the inside bend, where portages are usually located. The men found it easy going at the start and so were convinced they were on the right track. Then, fifteen minutes into the carry, they came upon a huge hill which was too rough to climb. The option was to backtrack to the head of the rapid, paddle cross the river and portage on the other side, or attempt a chancy ferry above the falls and run the narrow chute near the far shore (outside bend).

The crew chose to ferry and run—a big mistake. Their 17-foot long Old Town Tripper plunged over the falls and became pinned in the maelstrom below. Fortunately, both paddlers escaped without injury. Their friends, who were now at the base of the ledge, watched the scene unfold. Crushed by tons of water, the flattened and twisted Old Town eventually spit free and miraculously popped back into shape. It was recovered, minus some gear, in the pool below the rapid. Luckily, the damage—a broken thwart and tell-tale crease in the Royalex hull—was minimal.

The Answer: Probable Best Course of Action

If there's one cardinal rule in wilderness canoeing, it is: All canoes in a party should travel within sight of one another! Agree on a traveling philosophy before your trip, then stick to it!

2. A Local Concern

Scenario

Grand Rapids on the Mattagami River (northern Ontario) is more than a mile long and one-fourth as wide. When the water is high, the rapid is quite lively and produces a hollow drone which can be heard for miles. Nonetheless, the rapid is relatively easy if you choose the correct side of the river and stay alert. The rapid is indicated as a long series of hash marks on a 1:50,000 scale topo map.

A local resident offers advice as you and your partner are launching your canoe. He says to watch out for Grand Rapids! "There's a big ledge on the left that will eat you alive! Stay right and you'll be fine. It's been raining for weeks and the water's pretty high. I haven't canoed the stretch but I have fished it a lot. You guys be careful!"

The Question

You put ashore above the rapid, on the right bank, and cast a long look down stream. Huge rooster tails, far as the eye can see, present formidable obstacles. Maybe you can pick your way between the waves; maybe not. Hopefully, you search the jungle of head-high alders for signs of a portage. There is none!

From your vantage point, things look much better on the left side of the river. Indeed, you cannot see the ledge you were warned to avoid. But, it's a quarter mile to the other shore, and the current is very fast. An upstream ferry could be tricky. What to do?

Action Taken

The crew decided to run the rooster tails. Their 17-foot aluminum canoe capsized and wrapped around a rock. Unable to salvage their canoe or gear, the men abandoned their trip and walked the shoreline back to the town of Smoky Falls (about 30 miles), which took them three days.

The Answer: Probable Best Course Of Action

Always go with your gut feeling: If it doesn't look good, don't do it! The local fisherman said he was not a canoeist, and this admission should have invoked concerns. Also, the water was very high, which suggested unpredictable conditions. At worst, there could be dangerous keeper holes at the base of the ledge. At best, the ledge could be washed out and canoeable.

The team had three choices: they could have

1) checked the left side of the river for a safe route—running, lining and/or portaging as needed;

2) portaged and/or lined the right bank;

3) carefully scouted the rapid from the right shore, then canoed the safe portions and portaged or lined the rest. A pair of waterproof binoculars would have improved their rapid reading odds considerably.

3. A Vocal Local

Scenario

You are about to canoe the Steel River in northern Ontario. The MNR (Ministry of Natural Resources) trip guide indicates a three-quarter mile long portage that gains 400 feet of elevation in the first quarter mile(!). Paddlers who have done the Steel say that this Diablo Lake portage—which comes at the start of the trip—is a killer. But you and your friends have packed light and are paddling 40 pound solo canoes.

You have arranged with a local businessman to shuttle your car to the start of the route. As you are about to embark, the businessman pressures you to change your plans.

"Here's where you wanna start," he says, tapping his finger repeatedly on a point about five miles west of your intended put-in. "This here's a new trail— part of a 'Youth Works Project'. I've snowmobiled it dozens of times; it's a two lane highway and flat as a board."

You squint at the map. It's two, maybe three miles via this trail to Diablo Lake.

"Are you sure this trail is easier than the Diablo portage?" You ask.

"Hell, I live here, don't I?" comes the angry reply.

The Question

Should you tough it over the killer portage as planned, or carry two to three miles over the flats?

Action Taken

I made this canoe trip with friends in 1974, when few paddlers had heard of the Steel River or solo canoes. We followed the businessman's advice and took the YWP trail, which was anything but a two lane highway. Barely wide enough for our canoes, it was a tangled net of brush and downed trees. Unyieldingly, the path climbed steadily upward. It crossed two lakes, two beaver ponds and several swamps before it terminated at Diablo Lake, three miles away. We began the portage at 10 a.m. on a Sunday and reached Diablo Lake at noon, Monday!

The Answer: Probable Best Course of Action

I canoed the Steel River again in 1977. This time, I tried the MNR suggested route (Diablo portage). It was much easier. If there's a moral here, it is that the Ministry's advice is usually correct. MNR canoe trip guides are prepared by experienced canoeists who have done the trip and are familiar with the options.

Essentially, I trust the locals in matters related to road access, safe vehicle storage, availability of gasoline and other consumer services. However, I've learned that those who don't canoe don't understand canoes or canoeists, even if they live in the area! I rely on experienced wilderness paddlers who have been where I am going to answer questions about river logistics.

4. A Sick Situation

Scenario

You are canoeing a wild Canadian river, hundreds of miles from civilization, when your partner becomes seriously ill. She can't sit upright or retain food; her temperature is 102°F. There is no way she can paddle a canoe. You have been making poor time and are a full day behind schedule. You will rendezvous with your float plane one week from today.

High in the sky, wispy mares' tails suggest that a prolonged stretch of bad weather will reach you in 24 to 48 hours. There are a number of complex rapids ahead, which you don't want to paddle in rain. Today is warm and inviting; tomorrow, there will probably be wind and rain.

The Question

If you hole up and wait, you could miss the window you need to safely paddle the rapids. If you continue on, and capsize in a rapid, you risk the life of your partner, who is too sick to swim. You must make your rendezvous with the airplane. What to do?

Action Taken

The crew chose to lay over a day and give the sick woman a chance to recover. Rain came as expected and the crew stayed put a second day. They were now three days behind schedule and were worried they could not finish the trip on time. At noon, on the second layover day, the crew decided to continue the trip. They bundled the woman in warm clothes and made a bed for her in the bottom of a canoe. Then, they snapped the belly portion of the splash cover over her to keep out rain. Equipment was distributed among the other canoes. One canoe was cleared of packs so it could be paddled efficiently alone.

All canoes negotiated the rapids without incident, and the woman slept soundly throughout the experience. She awoke just as the hospital canoe emerged from the final drop of a complex rapid. She had no idea she had been canoeing white water. The crew was able to make up lost miles, and to complete their trip on time.

The Answer: Probable Best Course of Action

Although everything came out alright, this was not the best plan. A capsize could have been life-threatening to the sick person. It would have been better to lay over until the woman was strong enough to move about on her own steam, even if it meant missing the airplane.

Summer days are long (fourteen hours or more!) in northern Canada, so there's plenty of time to make up lost miles. Rapids and portages slow down the pace, and often create concern among paddlers. But, once on flatwater, good time—up to four miles an hour—may again be made. The crew lucked out in this scenario, even though they took some chances.

5. Inklings

Scenario

It's early June on a wild Canadian river you've paddled three times before. High water, low water, or in-between—no matter; you know every rock and curve by heart.

Round the bend you see the dancing horsetails of the 100 yard long rapid. It's tricky but you know just where to run it. Should you scout the drop from shore, or blindly make the run? Thick alders, with boulders in between, choke the banks to the water's edge, and there's a small island in the center of the river which you can't see around. Checking this rapid from both banks will take at least an hour. Fortunately, there are no trees nearby which could produce dangerous strainers, and the water is very low, so the rapid is less powerful than you remember it.

The Question

These are your options: You can blindly run the rapid, scout it from the right bank then run it; or ferry across the river and scout the left side. If you decide to shoot the rapid you must begin your descent near the right shore. Lining might be possible on the left bank, but not on the right. Portaging any portion of this drop is out-of-the-question.

Action Taken

The crew dutifully scouted the rapid from their location on the right shore. Everything looked okay. As they were about to make the run, pangs of conscience urged the exprienced leader to check the other side of the river. He did, and was horrified to discover that a two-inch trickle of water marked the vee of the always canoeable chute. He played out the scenario in his mind. Coming out of the fast-forward ferry, the canoe would spin downstream into nothingness and capsize in the heavy water that pounded the boulder line below. There simply wasn't enough water for a clean run!

The Answer: Probable Best Course of Action

A cardinal rule of canoeing is that you should scout every significant rapid before running it. Period! Rapids indicated on topographic maps usually rate high Class II or better. River characteristics change profoundly as water levels rise and fall—and generally, rapids on northern rivers become more difficult as they dry up.

As a trip wears on, even experienced paddlers tend to get lackadaisical about scouting rapids, especially those they have run before. But, with experience comes wisdom. Every canoeist has a river angel that whispers advice about dangers which lie ahead. Her message is constant, but fragile; it can be easily drowned out by previous success and the shrill of arrogance.

6. A Matter Of Privacy

Scenario

You have agreed to lead a co-ed group of teenagers on a canoe trip into the Boundary Waters Canoe Area of Minnesota. Some of the kids are concerned about the lack of privacy when going to the bathroom. They've been told that there is only one toilet per campsite (an exposed wooden or fiberglass box with a toilet seat on top) which must be shared by everyone. They've also heard that there are a few campsites on which potty's can sometimes be seen from portions of the tent area!

The Question

How can you ensure privacy and manage the potty so kids won't run into one another? You'll also need to make bathroom rules for areas in which there are no established toilets.

The Answer: Probable Best Course of Action

In areas where there are no established toilets, girls head off in one direction, boys go in another. They find a secluded spot that's at least 150 feet from water, then they dig a shallow hole with the heel of their boot. They do their thing in the hole then cover the hole with two or three inches of soil. That's all there is to it.

Human waste breaks down in a few weeks; toilet paper may require a season or more. For this reason, toilet paper is best burned before it is buried. However, teenagers can be careless—a toilet paper fire can get out-of-hand and create a dangerous situation! For this reason, only responsible adults (who have a water bottle handy) should burn their toilet paper. Teenagers, and everyone else, should just bury it!

On campsites, like those in the Boundary Waters, which have a designated non-private latrine, I follow this procedure:

Toilet paper is double-bagged in plastic and placed inside a bright-colored nylon bag, which is hung from a tree at the edge of camp. When someone has to use the latrine, he or she takes the toilet paper bag. No one hikes the trail to the latrine until the toilet paper bag is returned to the tree. This is one rule that kids take seriously!

If necessary, I hang a small plastic tarp in front of the latrine so it can't be seen from camp or the trail.

Note: Environmentalists agree that many small cat holes are better than one large latrine. However, not everyone is disciplined enough to dig holes and bury their wastes. For this reason, a well-maintained group toilet may be best when camping with large numbers of teenagers.

7. Drugged Up

Two True Scenarios

Scenario #1

You are in charge of a group of teenagers who are about to canoe a Canadian river. Everyone and everything will be bussed from the point of origin in the United States to the river. You pointedly remind participants that it is a serious customs violation to bring illegal drugs into Canada. Every child has signed an agreement which reads:

> Absolutely no tobacco, alcohol or drugs allowed on the canoe trip. If I am caught with an illegal substance during the drive to Canada, I will be OFF THE TRIP immediately! I will be taken to the nearest police station, where I will be held until my parents pick me up! If, during the course of the canoe trip, it is discovered that I have drugs in my possession, I will be reported to the police in my hometown after the trip. I will accept whatever punishment I receive, and in addition, I will do thirty hours of community service.

The Question

You are at a highway rest stop, 300 miles from home, when a student tells you that John has some joints. At the next rest stop you call John aside. Sure enough, he has the makings for a half dozen marijuana cigarettes. You are shocked because John is one of the nicest kids on the trip. He's a straight-A student, a good leader, and he's always kind and considerate. His parents are wonderful and they actively support your canoeing program. You can't believe that John, of all people, got busted.

John cries hippopotamus tears and says he's never done anything illegal before. He apologizes profusely and promises to make amends during and after the trip. "Just please let me go on the canoe trip," he begs.

Here are your options:

1. Confiscate the drugs, accept John's apology and allow him to go on the canoe trip. Assign heavy camp chores (dish-washing, wood-cutting, etc.) as punishment. Call John's parents when you get home.

2. Stick to your guns: call his parents immediately and drop him off at the nearest police station.

3. Work out a compromise: maybe call John's parents now, then let him go on the trip. Or, ask the other kids to come up with a plan. Cutting John from the trip will mean reorganizing gear and paddling teams. It will be a nightmare.

Scenario #2

Same as scenario #1 except the drugs are discovered at a wilderness campsite on the second day of your canoe trip.

The Question:

What's your plan of action?

Action Taken: Scenario #1

The leader—a 35 year old Junior High School teacher—empathized with John and accepted his apology. Then he took the boy to the nearest police station, where the boy called his parents and waited for them to pick him up.

The Answer: Probable Best Course of Action—#1

The teacher stuck to his guns, which is always the best plan when working with teenagers. Fortunately, the parents were also cooperative. John learned an important lesson, and as far as I know he never again did anything unlawful.

Action Taken: Scenario #2

The leader confiscated the drugs and told the youngster that his parents and the local police would be notified after the trip. The boy was genuinely sorry and asked if he could perform his thirty hours of community service during the course of the canoe trip. "I'll cut wood and wash dishes, carry canoes, make fires, cook—anything," pleaded the boy. The leader agreed to the proposal and everyone—except the boy—had a very relaxing canoe trip.

The Answer: Probable Best Course of Action—#2

Tripping camps that specialize in treating juvenile delinquents commonly use hard camp work (chopping wood, hauling water, etc.) as a consequence for bad behavior. In this case, however, it probably was a bad idea because it modified the experience of the non-delinquent kids. A canoe trip is a group endeavor, and a wilderness learning situation. Everyone should have had a hand in cutting wood, hauling water and other tough chores. But, the bad boy did the lion's share, and as a result, may have been the only one on that canoe trip who learned humility and the meaning of hard work. The child should have done his thirty hours of community service in the community, not on the canoe trip!

8. Fire In The Sky

Scenario

You're canoeing a small river when a fierce storm suddenly blows up. Rain comes down in sheets and lightning dances violently across the sky. You determine the distance of the strike from your location by counting the seconds between the lightning flash and thunder boom. Then, you divide this figure by five to get an answer in miles.

The strike is now a mile away and getting closer. BOOM!..one, one thousand, two, one thous...FLASH! Two-and-one-half seconds divided by five equals half a mile. Things are heating up fast!

The Question

At this rate, a lightning strike could be upon you in minutes. You must take action now. Consider this before you decide what to do:

- The river is barely fifty yards wide and you are located right in the middle of it!

- Tall trees line the banks, right to the water's edge.

- The brushy shoreline suggests that it won't be easy to find a good place to land.

- There is no distinct high or low ground. Everything within walking (running!) distance is at nearly the same elevation.

- It is raining so hard that you can barely see your partner, let alone the river banks.

- There are no rapids ahead.

Action Taken

I was canoeing the Gull River in Ontario when the lightning scenario developed. At the two-and-one-half-second strike, my friend, Al Todnem, turned his red Mad River canoe sharply towards shore and paddled for dear life. I stayed put in the middle of the river and yelled for him to come back, but he couldn't hear me above the roar of the storm.

Al's canoe was just off shore when lightning struck a tall birch tree at the river's edge. The top exploded into flame and sparks showered in all directions. The severed—and actively burning—tree top splashed down within feet of the red canoe. Lucky it missed, because it must have weighed half a ton! Then, an acrid smell of ozone pierced the air, and suddenly, the woods were afire!

I'll never forget the look of horror on Al's face as he paddled back to me. He knew he was lucky to be alive!

The Answer: Most Probable Course Of Action

The advice to get off the water when lightning strikes is sound, provided there's a safe landing spot—and a low, lightning-protected place nearby. In this case, there was no safe haven. Tall trees lined the shore, which suggested lightning might strike there first. It did! In this case, the center of the river was the safest place to be. Here's why:

A cone-of-protection extends from the tallest object about 45 degrees in all directions. The best plan is to stay within this protected zone, but not so close to its center that lightning may jump to you. Lightning can jump 30 feet or more; so 50-100 feet from shore may be the best place to be. The narrowness of this river, the adjacent high trees, and the lack of a lightning-protected spot, suggested that the shoreline could be dangerous. It was!

9. Fancy Feet

Scenario

You are planning a canoe trip down a remote northern river which flows to Hudson Bay. Timing is critical: If you leave too early in the season, you may be stopped by ice; if you start too late, there may not be enough water to float your canoe. You are scheduled to leave within days of ice-out to ensure the best canoeing conditions. However, you've heard that even when the water is high, there are long, shallow stretches which require wading in ice cold water.

You are an experienced leader and have provided everyone in your crew with an equipment list which specifies these items:

- 16-inch high rubber boots (a must!). Be sure your boots are large enough accept warm insoles.
- Two pairs of warm insoles for your rubber boots (a must!).
- One pair of leather boots or tennis shoes for camp use. A pair of wet-suit socks or Gore-Tex®. socks that fit inside the boots may be useful.

The Question

On the first day of your canoe trip you encounter a long shallow rapid that must be waded. The water is bitterly cold and you observe that one person is wearing Gore-Tex® socks inside sneakers, instead of the recommended rubber boots. Is she warm enough? Time will tell.

Day three of your canoe trip and the wading continues. The bootless woman has stopped smiling. Her Gore-Tex® socks are torn and her feet are cold. What to do?

Here are some things to consider:

1. You don't like wet feet so you've brought along an extra pair of waterproof boots—a tall pair of Tingley® rubber overshoes which you can put on if you go over the tops of your 16-inch high rubber boots. The flexible rubber Tingley's weigh less than a pound and take up less pack space than a pair of walking shoes. You can wear the Tingley's alone with heavy socks or a felt liner, or in combination with your sneakers. It would be a nice gesture if you loaned

your Tingley's to the woman.

2. Don't lend your Tingley's to the woman; it's her problem, not yours! High-top rubber boots were listed a *must* item. The woman chose not to bring them along.

3. Help the woman repair her leaking Gore-Tex® socks.

4. Stop and rest frequently–give the woman a chance to dry and warm her wet feet.

Action Taken

The Tingley® boots were reluctantly offered to the cold-footed lady, who was very grateful to receive them. But, as time wore on, the rapids worsened and the weather turned sour. By the end of the first week, everyone in the crew had cold, wet feet, and the gracious provider of the boots secretly wanted them back. Eventually, an air of hushed unfriendliness developed between the provider and recipient. Fortunately, the woman sensed the tension and returned the boots. The provider—who now felt guilty for being so selfish— apologized profusely then made some waterproof socks from large poly bags which, incidentally, worked surprisingly well. Two days later, the sun came out and dried everyone's feet and brightened their attitude.

The Answer: Most Probable Course Of Action

The strong recommendation that everyone bring rubber boots should not have gone ignored. The woman made her own bed and she should have slept in it. Most wilderness experts would probably agree that the Tingley's should have been offered only if the woman's health or functional ability was impaired. In this case, it wasn't. Yes, she had cold feet. But, on occasion, so did everyone else. More importantly, there was no danger of frostbite or hypothermia—and, there was always a roaring fire in camp at the end of the day. It's not fair that the one person who planned for a worst case scenario was penalized for thinking ahead.

Everyone is responsible for their own comfort on a canoe trip. Essential items were clearly spelled out on the equipment list. The woman simply chose not to bring them.

This was clearly a painful learning experience, not a life-threatening one. Victims of a canoe capsize, wind-shredded tent or other misfortune need immediate help—which should be given without question or concern for one's own well-being. However, an unplanned disaster is one thing; reluctance to follow the clear directions of an experienced leader is another!

10. Life Jacket

Scenario

Sunrise on a wilderness canoe trip. The crew crowds around the breakfast fire and takes a long, hard look at the map. For at least the next two days, there are rapids—lots of 'em! And the easiest looks mighty challenging. Slowly, concerns merge to smiles as everyone re-affirms his or her own paddling skills and agrees that "the rapids are what they came for."

Reluctantly, one man sheepishly announces that he left his life jacket on a rock at yesterday's lunch spot. Then, he buries his head in his hands and says, "I'm not a very good swimmer."

A horrified look flashes across the faces of the crew. Everyone knows there are big rapids ahead. It would be unthinkable to do them without a PFD (personal flotation device), even if one is a good swimmer!

The Question

Going back for the life jacket will take at least two days. There's a large lake to cross, then a two mile portage, followed by six miles of shallow but determined rapids which can't be lined. What to do? Formulate a plan that everyone can live with.

Action Taken

The crew followed this plan whenever they encountered a testy rapid: The most experienced team ran the drop first. They put ashore at the base of the pitch and carried a life jacket back to the man who had lost his. The other canoes just hung around until the life jacket arrived, and the delivery men had returned to their canoe. Now, everyone was prepared for an upset, and there was a rescue boat in a convenient location at the bottom of the rapid.

The Answer: Most Probable Course of Action

Retracing the route with hopes of finding the lost life jacket probably would have been a waste of energy and time. If the vest was left on an obscure rock as the man stated, the crew would be lucky to find it! In this instance, sharing a life jacket was the right plan because the rapids were well defined and had good trails around them. It would have been out of the question if shorelines were impassable—which is often the case on northern rivers. Losing a life jacket is so serious that some canoe parties carry a spare.

Should a good swimmer have offered his or her life jacket to the poor swimmer who lost his? Probably not. Canoeists who don't wear life jackets risk drowning, even if they are excellent swimmers. This crew made a very wise decision!

11. LOST!

Scenario

Eight experienced canoeists are camped at a picturesque site along the Seal River in remote, northern Manitoba. It's seven p.m. and the cook announces that supper will be ready at nine. He suggests that those who are not involved with preparing the meal get lost for a couple hours.

Excited at the opportunity for some free time, six people decide to go exploring. Two strike out together in one direction; the rest go their separate ways. Unbeknown to the group leader, no one brings a map, compass, matches or a flashlight.

The Question

Nine o'clock approaches and the explorers haven't returned. Yelling produces no response. At 9:30, the light begins to fade and there's still no sign of anyone. The two men in camp have a whistle, three orange smoke signals, two 15-second flares, a high-powered rifle, compass, map and a battery-powered GPS. A cheery fire has been burning for hours.

You're the group leader: what should you do?

Action Taken

The fire was piled high and the whistle was blown continually for several minutes. No effect. Around 9:30, darkness began to close in and the leader became seriously worried. After all, the area was very remote and the closest human settlement was Churchill, Manitoba, over 100 air miles away!

A study of the map revealed that camp was located on the tip of a narrow peninsula, which in low water might become an island. If the hikers were on the peninsula they should have heard the whistle. If they were on the mainland, they were probably lost and out of whistle range. The narrow bottle-neck which led to camp would be very difficult to find in failing light.

The leader figured it was too dark to see an orange smoke signal, and he was reluctant to fire a flare overhead for fear it might land in the bush and start a forest fire. He reasoned that if he shot a flare out over the river it could mis-lead the hikers and cause them to bypass the peninsula which led to camp. He also questioned whether the flares would burn long enough to be seen by the hikers. He decided to save the flares as a last resort.

Around 10 p.m., the fading light turned to darkness. Still, no hikers. The two men in camp had yelled themselves hoarse and were tired of blowing whistles and banging on pots. With high hopes, the pair kept piling wood on the already three-foot high bon-fire.

Finally, the leader brought out the high-powered rifle and slowly fired three shots into the air. He repeated this twice more, at ten minute intervals. It was amazing how loud the rifle sounded as it echoed across the water. "Surely, they can hear this," he muttered hopefully.

They did! The six explorers wandered into camp shortly after the last shot was fired.

They explained that they had all become lost, but had somehow run into one another. They said they thought they once heard the whistle, but it was so far away they couldn't place the direction. The loud crack of the rifle was what brought them in.

"Think you guys would have seen a flare?" asked the leader. "I doubt it," said one man, "We were in pretty thick woods."

The Answer: Best Probable Course of Action

Experienced hikers would naturally ask why each person didn't have a map and compass. A compass, certainly! But seldom does everyone on a Canadian canoe trip have their own map set. Canadian quadrangles cost around eight dollars a piece—a full map set often runs over 100 dollars! For this reason, canoe partners usually share one set of maps. The sheets are zipped or taped inside a waterproof map case, and are often quite bulky—not something you'd want to carry on a casual hike. Breaking up a map set—to take a pertinent sheet—is often a hassle. Of course, a complete map set is required equipment on every hike the group takes together.

In this scenario, the hikers were all experienced so the leader didn't bother to check (he should have!) to see if they each had a compass, whistle and flashlight, and a knowledge of their location. He should have suggested that it was getting late, so they should probably travel together and carry a map. He might have have even programmed the location of the camp into the GPS and given the GPS to the crew. This would have been the best plan, for the GPS, with its back-lit screen, would have brought everyone home in the black of night.

It was probably wise not to shoot off the flares. It was almost too dark to travel when the hikers arrived. If the group was out of hearing range of the rifle shots, it's doubtful that one or two 15-second flares would bring them in. In the morning, the leader could light an orange smoke signal. The smoke should be visible for miles. If that didn't bring results, a GPS-coordinated search along marked grid lines would be the next step.

12. An Heroic Rescue

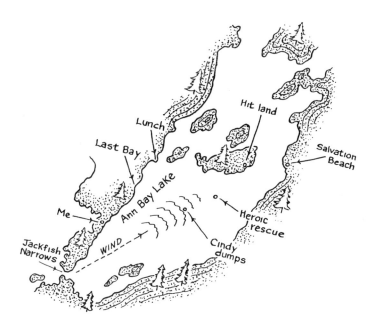

The following life-threatening experience took place on the Turtle River in northern Ontario. The Turtle is not a particularly difficult canoe route. The rapids are short and well-defined, and the portages are generally good. The major obstacle is a number of large sprawling lakes which you must navigate and which demand attention if the wind is up. Experienced Boundary Waters and Quetico Park canoeists—who have good judgment and basic whitewater skills —would find themselves right at home on the Turtle River.

I am departing from the usual format of this book to allow Jim Leavitt to share his story with you in his own words. I hope you will frequently pause to consider each decision that Jim made. And lest you judge Jim's actions too harshly, be aware that he and his wife, Cindy are superb whitewater paddlers and very competent outdoors people. I've paddled three tough Canadian Rivers with Jim and Cindy and they have earned my respect. The Leavitt's have good judgment— they know they can't beat the river. Jim is an experienced physician in Eau Claire, Wisconsin, and Cindy is a Registered nurse. Both know the dangers of cold water and hypothermia.

Jim and Cindy's story depicts a scenario that has been repeated thousands of times in thousands of places all over the world. It points out how one small mistake can be life-threatening, and how one bad choice can lead to another. Most important, it illustrates that there are no pat formulas for correcting a serious error.

Every experienced canoeist I know has had at least one potentially life-threatening experience. It's part of the learning curve. However, most paddlers are simply too embarrassed to admit their mistakes. Jim Leavitt is a notable exception. I commend Jim and thank him for allowing me to share his story with you.

To encourage you to think carefully about options, I've inserted (What would you do next?) at key places in the copy. Make your choice, then read on to see what happened. You'll discover that things complicate quickly after the initial disaster. Hindsight here is a perfect 20:20!

The Setting

As told by Jim Leavitt

August, 1995—Two canoes—myself and a male friend in a 174 Old Town Discovery canoe, and Cindy and a lady friend in an 18' We-no-nah Sundowner canoe. It was the fifth day of a week-long trip which started at Turtle Lake, North of Atikokan, Ontario.

We were greeted by a very strong headwind on White Otter Lake which slowed our progress considerably (map, figure 12). To conserve energy, we would paddle hard from bay to bay, rest a moment and go on. We were pleased that we were able to negotiate the difficult wind tunnel between the large north-south island and the west shore. We stopped for lunch at a small protected sand beach.

(What would you do next?)

Decision #1

Our lunch spot was small but comfortable and, if need be, we could have camped there for the night. However, I was disappointed that we hadn't come as far that day as I'd hoped. I wanted to make a beautiful campsite at the south end of Ann Bay at Jackfish Narrows. Besides, we had, I thought, easily made it across the roughest part of the lake.

We were confidently jumping from bay to bay and had come around another small point to run along the west shore into the wind. My Old Town Discovery made the move without difficulty and we went about one kilometer down the shore to wait for Cindy and her friend in the Sundowner. The two were in trouble as soon as they rounded the point—the more they tried to turn towards shore, the more they were blown out to sea. I watched their lack of progress from shore and assumed that, with a little more time and effort, they would soon join us, even though I could see they were moving farther out into the lake.

I left my companion on shore to watch them with binoculars, while I climbed the cliff and searched for a campsite. Twenty minutes later I returned and could barely see them with binoculars. Occasionally I caught a flash of white out on the lake which suggested that the canoe had tipped over and was rolling repeatedly in the waves.

Now, what do I do?

(What would you do next?)

Decision #2

A) Go after them!

B) Stay where I am knowing that they are both foundering in heavy water far from shore?

Cynthia is not a strong swimmer so I was very worried. Even though the water was relatively warm, it could be several hours before the capsized canoe washed ashore. It was a little after one o'clock, so the wind would continue to blow for many more hours.

C) Work my way north along the shore, behind the two islands, so I could pick them up more quickly when the wind settled down?

I entertained this thought for a few seconds but didn't give it much weight. Precious time was slipping by. I was even more worried that I wouldn't be able to see them from the north side of the islands.

(What would you do next?)

I went after them! A tiny voice inside me told me it was unlikely I would succeed, and that if both canoes swamped I couldn't help myself or anyone else. Besides, there was no guarantee that the two swamped canoes would drift together in the same direction. This was a huge lake, with lots of bays and potential landing spots. If I lost sight of them I might not find them again! However, I had an overwhelming feeling that I must do something, even if it was foolish.

Adding to this was my partner who could not swim and said, "I don't want to die!"

(What would you do next?)

Question

Do I go out with a loaded or an empty canoe?

A. Empty.

I knew that I could probably control the canoe better if it was light. The craft would also sit higher in the water and be less likely to swamp from the following seas.

B. Loaded.

My concern was leaving our only known dry gear—two tents and clothing plus stoves—behind on the shore at such a distance that I could not retrieve them before dark. I had no way of knowing if Cindy's packs had remained with the canoe or floated free. If they were gone, I would need my equipment to rig a comfortable camp. But, it would be a disaster if I also tipped over and lost everything. What to do?

(What would you do next?)

I went out loaded. I decided to go straight into the middle of the lake then head northeast with the wind behind me. I knew that a following sea is much more dangerous than a head wind. However, there was no choice; I'd have to run with the waves at my tail. The stern of the canoe began to weather-vane as soon as it broke into the waves, so I put ashore and readjusted the load so the tail was heavier than the bow. This solved the problem.

However, by the time I finished re-trimming the boat, I could not see the other canoe. I guessed they were two or three miles away. I turned down-wind and started for the far diagonal shore, thinking this is where they were headed. About half-way down the lake my bow partner spotted them to the northwest. I had erred too far east. It took two Z maneuvers to re-align my canoe with theirs. The wind was blowing stronger than ever and I was surprised we didn't tip over when we made the turns.

Minutes later we intercepted the swamped canoe and were relieved to see that Cindy and her friend were hanging on to the boat. Thank God they were both wearing life jackets! All the gear and paddles were gone. The flash of light I saw on shore was the canoe rolling in the heavy waves. I estimated they had been in the water for nearly an hour. The women were cold but not hurt.

(What would you do next?)
Now what do I do?

A. *Try to empty the canoe and right it (canoe-over-canoe rescue).*
No way! Not in these waves.

B. *Have them hold onto their boat and tow it with ours.*
The swamped canoe was acting like a large sea anchor, so I guessed our canoe would probably just wallow in the waves until it swamped. Trash this idea.

C. *Have them hold onto the stern line or side of our canoe while we towed them ashore.*
Tried this, but had the same wallowing sea anchor effect.

D. *Ask them to let go of their boat and climb aboard ours.*
We chose option **D**. Miraculously, we got them both into the middle of the canoe from opposite sides—not without some anxious moments, like when Cindy's partner got her leg stuck between the wanigan and gunnel and couldn't get all the way in or remove her leg. I knew that if she lost her grip on the center thwart she would fall off the gear and possibly break her leg and drown. If she fell, she wouldn't be able to extract her leg and I would need to roll the canoe over and dump us all. Fortunately, I was able to get her leg free and her into the canoe.

I was able to hold this unstable construct together for only about fifteen minutes before we capsized!

There are now four adults and a load of camping gear in a capsized canoe, in a heaving sea.

(What would you do next?)

A. *Hold onto our canoe and float.*
We tried it and barely moved at all!

B. *Hold on to the canoe and kick with our feet.*
We tried this, to no avail. No effect with Bean boots—and I didn't want to lose them.

C. Let go of the canoe and float with either our life jackets or a gear pack or wanigan?

This would get us out of the water more quickly and thereby minimize the effects of hypothermia. However, all four of us might be scattered across a large shoreline with no canoe or gear. And if we did all make it to the same spot, there would be no dry clothes, food or equipment. If we left the canoes we might never find them again. What to do?

D. Try to paddle!

(What would you do next?)

Paddling seemed the best alternative. I hoped to make it to the big island but the alignment of the canoe suggested that, without forward progress, it would drift past the corner and head down the lake. I had three paddles in my boat—so with one person holding onto a tent which had popped out from beneath a Duluth flap, and the other three standing in the bow, stern and center, we began to awkwardly paddle. It seemed to serve several purposes; gave us something to do in the face of utter helplessness; warmed us up; and maybe, just maybe brought us closer to land. I knew that if we missed the island, we would float for hours at the mercy of the waves. Hypothermia and progressive despair wouldn't allow us to be in the water much longer. It required constant chatter and encouragement to keep from giving up. It was frightening to hear someone say, "I can't go on."

I set the boat on a quartering tack and we seemed to make progress. But as soon as we'd get ahead a wave would roll us over. When we were standing in the canoe, the water was waist high. Sitting would have been better except that the waves were so high they washed over us and prevented us from paddling.

We finally hit the island just past an almost vertical rock wall. The women had been in the water for nearly four hours. Cindy was visibly blue and shaking and was not responding to verbal cues. Hypothermia had set in!

Equipment on hand included two personal packs, one wanigan with pantry goods, two day packs and pack basket—enough to make fire and rig a snug camp.

The shore on which we landed was so rocky and overgrown that we could barely sit or stand. Camping was impossible. Fortunately, one of my two PEAK 1 stoves worked. I had an emergency fire starting kit in my thwart bag and soon got a large blaze going. Modesty took a back seat to a swift change of clothes.

(What would you do next?)

A No Choice Decision

We had to get off the rocks. Once re-warmed, it was time to move. But how? Four people in one canoe was out of the question, so I put three people and two articles of gear in the boat and struck out for the far shore. The wind was diminishing, and so was my self-confidence. I simply did not want to paddle in any waves!

The good part of the catastrophe was the sandy beach towards which we were headed. There was a gentle slope, enough room for a dozen tents, and plenty of firewood. And wonder of wonders—we found one Duluth pack and the gear Wanigan lying on the beach! We were still missing the food pack and one personal pack, but we did have four live humans, one canoe, three paddles and enough food and gear to get by. My psyche was so fragile that I waited an hour before I returned to pick up the remaining person. Now, all waves looked too menacing!

The rest is history: A roaring fire was built and dinner was scrounged from the pantry. Without sleeping bags for all of us, it was a miserable night for some.

It's amazing how, in a catastrophe, your world narrows to a few basic needs. What I wanted most was a second canoe. The area was fairly remote, so I knew that we could sit on this beach for days—maybe weeks—before we were found. Staying put was not an option. I would rather move as a group than divide up.

Earlier that evening, I saw the second canoe blow down the lake. It was headed towards a huge 40 meter vertical rock face about one kilometer from our camp. Would it break up on the rocks or drift into a quiet eddy? I hoped I would not be packing the Sundowner home in a Duluth pack!

(What would you do next?)

A miracle! The next morning we found the canoe at the base of the rock face, with a sharp vertical edge jutting from the water. It was intact, except for two symmetrical four inch holes in the rails. Now, if I could just find another paddle...

I no longer cared about the food pack or missing Duluth pack. I just wanted out of there! We emptied the We-no-nah and towed it back to camp. Further down the sand beach, I discovered a paddle. What joy!

Epilogue

That morning we found the other two paddles and remaining packs scattered along the beach. The only losses were one pair of boots, a hat and towel. To our good fortune, the sun was shining and everything was dry by noon. We made 14 km. by evening and found a nice campsite close to the final portage.

I can attest that Cliff Jacobson's bagging system does keep everything dry, even when packs are attached to thwarts and agitated in a heaving lake for more than a day.

What I Learned

- Don't try to swim while wearing **Bean** boots.

- When in doubt, stay put!

- A submerged PEAK 1 stove will fire up with a little encouragement.

- If you don't have a doubt, you're not considering all the possibilities!

- People are important, gear is expendable!

The Answer: In Respectful Retrospect

Jim Leavitt's crew successfully crossed the roughest part of Ann Bay, so Jim reasonably figured that they should have been able to handle the rest without difficulty.

Any prudent canoeist might have made the same judgment call and duplicated Jim's experience. Nonetheless, I would have had two concerns:

#1. Before making the final crossing I would have re-trimmed each canoe so it wouldn't weather-vane on the down-wind run. Then, I would have told the second canoe to stay within shouting distance of my canoe. All canoes in a party should stay together when crossing a windy lake, even if it means that the fast team must slow down. Not all canoeists are strong paddlers, and not all canoes are equally fast. Getting ahead—way ahead—of your friends on a wind-blown lake minimizes the chances of a successful rescue.

Admittedly, under real field conditions it's not easy to slow down a fast team. Some of the speed is macho; some of it is wind-driven exhilaration; and most, perhaps, is just the desire to get out of danger as quickly as possible. Nonetheless, canoes should stay together when things get rough. Had Jim been closer to Cindy when the capsize occurred, he might have approached the problem differently. The water was relatively warm so hypothermia would not have been an immediate concern.

#2. Those who are familiar with canoes will recognize that the Old Town 17'4" Discovery and 18' We-no-nah Sundowner, are vastly different craft. The Sundowner is designed for fast, efficient travel on open rivers and Boundary Waters style lakes. It turns reluctantly in currents and wind, and its narrow bow tends to submarine in huge waves. The Sundowner is a fine canoe but it's not the best one for the Canadian bush.

The Discovery on the other hand is a marginally sluggish general purpose canoe, that has no virtues or faults. It turns better and is much more forgiving than the Sundowner. Note that Jim had to make several Z turns to get to Cindy's swamped canoe. He might not have been able to make the turns in the Sundowner.

Am I suggesting that the Sundowner is inferior to the Discovery? Not a chance. Both canoes have their place. The Sundowner was simply out of its element here. The roles might have been reversed if Cindy had been paddling the Discovery.

This is not a matter of which canoe is best. It's a matter of knowing—and complying with—the capabilities of all the craft in your party. Had Jim been paddling the more sporty Sundowner, he might never have attempted the crossing.

Rule: all canoes in a party should be matched to the task. Tone down your expectations if they're not!

In Search of Cindy

No experienced paddler I know would fault Jim Leavitt for going after his wife. His decision to go out loaded was correct, both for the reason he cited, and to increase ballast and control in the waves. I would have moved all gear as close to the center of the canoe as possible. Then, I would have positioned my partner behind the bow seat and assumed a kneeling position against the rear thwart. This would have lightened the ends of the canoe and produced a drier, more controllable ride.

The Heroic Rescue

I would argue against putting four people in the canoe. Jim knew this would result in disaster, and it did. I would choose one of these options:

a) Command the paddlers to grab the stern line of my canoe, roll over on their backs (their heads towards the stern of my canoe) and kick hard with their feet to provide some forward motion. I would then point the canoe about 20 degrees into the wind (tacking route) and paddle aggressively. Hopefully, we would make some headway. If not, I'd try option **b** which, I think, is probably the best.

b) One paddler straddles the bow of my canoe, the other straddles the stern. The paddlers lay on their backs, their feet locked over the rails of the canoe. They hold tight to the canoe and lift themselves out of the water as much as possible. Their life jackets should support their torso. Now, the canoe is in balance and the swimmers are essentially part of the canoe. This is an effective rough water rescue procedure. I agree with Jim that under these conditions the Boy Scout canoe-over-canoe rescue technique is out-of-the-question.

c) Paddlers in, packs out! One could clip the dumped packs (they'd float) to the stern line, then tow them behind the canoe. The packs would act much like a sea anchor and slow the canoe down, but three people paddling might overcome the drag.

As you can see, once the initial mistake is made, everything that follows centers around making the best of a bad situation. In this scenario, cool-headedness and dogged determination saved the day. In another situation this may be not enough.

It's interesting to note that Jim's conscience told him to remain at the safe lunch spot until the wind died down. But he ignored the warning.

My advice? Keep your group together, consider the worst case scenario and always go with your gut feeling. And don't allow a tight schedule or friends to pressure you into doing something that you know is unsafe.

13. Animal Protection Device

Frequently Asked Question

"I'm going to the Boundary Waters next summer for the first time. I hear there are bears about! How do I protect myself from these critters? Should I bring a gun or some mace? It's 102° here in Oklahoma and I want to go up north and paddle where it's cool. But I don't want to get eaten alive by a hungry bear! Please help!"

Also, my sister is a crazy canoe nut. She's canoeing the Seal River to Hudson Bay this summer, and will be flying in on some dinky little float plane. The pilot says to watch out for polar bears! Sis and I fight a lot, but I still love her. I don't want her to die on this canoe trip! I've got an old shotgun she can use but Sis has never fired a gun. What to do?

Bearly Scared in Tulsa

The Answer

Dear Bearly Scared:

Calm down. The likelihood you'll be eaten by a bear is small—about the same as being struck by lightning in the Gobi desert. However, there are some precautions you'll want to take. But first, you must understand the differences between black bears, polar bears and grizzly bears. In a nutshell:

Black Bears

Black bears are usually very timid. They'll run at the first sight (or smell!) of you. Don't corner one or come between a sow and her cubs. And don't run away—the bear will chase you for sure! Attacks are rare. Most attacks are really bluff charges—the bear runs towards you and makes scary noises. World famous bear ecologist Lynn Rogers says that you can almost always stop a bluff charge if you hold your ground, spread your arms wide (so you look real big!) and loudly yell, "Whoa bear!" Lynn claims the bear will usually stop a few arm lengths away! Strangely enough, I refuse to test the idea.

Admittedly, it requires a cool head to stand your ground and yell. An alternative is to spray the bear with a mace-like product that contains oleo capsaicin pepper—the flaming ingredient in red pepper. This should stop him immediately without doing physical damage.

Please note that bear mace and human mace are not the same. The animal variety—which contains ten percent pepper—is a different mix, and much more powerful than the human type. The large size, one-pound can sprays up to thirty feet; pocket sized models go half as far and deliver less pepper. Get the largest can you can find! And do get a belt holster. Bear mace won't do you any good if it's locked away in your pack.

Quite honestly, you don't need bear mace in the BWCA. However, you might find it useful in New York or Los Angeles. By the way, mace is illegal in Canada, but animal protection devices are not. If the cayenne-based product has a picture of a bear on the label and is clearly labeled for use on animals, it's legal in Canada. Bear mace is available at many outdoor stores and at some western U.S. national park shops. Or, you may order it direct from Caldwell enterprises[1]. My wife, Susie accidentally triggered a split second burst of Counter Assault® in her mother's kitchen. Her dad was sleeping upstairs. Seconds later he was coughing and his eyes were watering. The home had to be evacuated for two hours! The product works!

If a black bear attacks you, fight with all your might. Do not play dead! Predacious bear attacks usually occur in daylight, and when the victim is alone. If a black bear comes into your camp at night, it's probably because he is too chicken to face you in daylight. There is safety in numbers: it is almost unheard of for a black bear to attack a group of six or more people.

Grizzly Bears

Grizzlies are ordinarily very shy. Consider yourself lucky if you see one. They are very possessive of their territory (like favorite fishing spots), and are somewhat nearsighted, so they often charge in fast to see what's going on.

Example: When I canoed the Hood River, N.W.T. in 1984, I was charged by three grizzlies on the open tundra. The bears came within fifty feet, caught my smell and bolted away. They were fat and sassy and had been eating caribou. Thank goodness I didn't look or smell like one!

I canoed the Hood again in 1992 and observed a similar experience. Two men were obliviously fishing from their canoe, which had grounded on a small sandbar in an eddy below a powerful falls, when the grizzly came toward them. Curious about the intruders, the bear loped easily at them, coming to an abrupt halt just two canoe lengths away. Momentarily, men and beast stood frozen as they faced one another. Then, suddenly, the bruin turned and galloped full speed away as fast as his powerful legs could carry him.

Rule: If you are charged by a grizzly, roll into the fetal position (hands clasped behind your neck) and play stone dead. Do not run or try to do battle with a grizzly bear! Bear mace will almost always stop a grizzly. I always carry a can when I canoe tundra rivers.

Polar Bears

The North Knife River in Manitoba flows to Hudson Bay. My journal entry for July 20, 1992 reads as follows:

Coming around a bend, my partner Joanie points and says, "Hey, Cliff, look at that mountain goat up there." Seconds later the goat transmutes into a full-grown male polar bear, who slides down the bank and swims straight toward our canoe.

"Backferry!" I yell. "Jesus Christ, backferry!" It's like we're paddling through glue, and the bear keeps coming! Luckily, when he's barely fifty feet away, the powerful current sweeps him around the bend. Will he come ashore and crash back through the bush at us? Soon as the boat touches land, I'm out, rifle in hand and praying I won't have to shoot. Seconds later, Dick and Finette arrive, sheet white. Suddenly, it turns into a comedy—everyone massed in a tiny group, scared as hell, me clutching the half-cocked .444 Marlin while Dick drops shotgun slugs into the sand... We're seventy-five miles from the bay and no one but me is ready to shoot. What a rush!

Saw three more bears later—two swimming, one on land. Bear tracks everywhere. We arranged tents like a fort. Perimeter teams have bear mace. I served everyone double shots of Pusser's rum tonight!"

Polar Bears II

Polar bears are not shy and they are not afraid of anything. They are very curious, confident and matter-of-fact. Where a grizzly will run in for a closer look, a polar bear will walk in. If he likes what he sees, he'll start chomping away. If not, he'll do a lazy 180° and slowly amble away, stopping frequently to assess the situation. Polar bears are like cats: they make no sounds on land or water. Most of the people who have survived a polar bear attack never heard or saw the bear coming! A big bear can swim several hundred miles in ice water at speeds up to six miles an hour. That's faster than I can paddle my canoe!

Capsaicin spray will put down a polar bear. However, you're most apt to encounter polar bears where there are no trees to break the wind. If the breeze is wrong when you trigger the spray, you might accidentally mace yourself! For this reason, a gun is more reliable in polar bear bear country, if it is available and you know how to use it!

A pump-action, twelve gauge shotgun is the firearm of choice. Place three slugs into the magazine, followed by two plastic stinger slugs. Stinger slugs are similar to those used by police to control riots. They have a velocity of 635 feet per second, a range of about sixty meters, and accuracy enough to hit a water bucket at fifty yards.

If a bear comes close, shoot him (take care to avoid the head) several times with the plastic stinger slugs. He will almost always go away. Lethal lead is available if he doesn't. Another tier of protection is to shoot a fire-cracker shell at the bear when you first see him. Fire-cracker shells loudly explode on impact and will usually scare a curious bear away. Your state wildlife management agency can tell you where to get them.

Caution: Practice with fire-cracker shells before you use them. If the cracker shell explodes behind the bear rather than in front of him, you're in big trouble!

Plastic stinger shells are available from AAI Corporation, P.O. Box 126, Hunt Valley, MD 21030. They are dubbed BD-100, or simply BEAR, which stands for Best Ecological Alternative Round. They come packed five to a box and cost about five dollars per shell.

And now to your final question: Should you give Sis your gun? Yes, if she will take time to learn to use it. No, if she won't! Bear mace is a safer option. I consider it essential on any canoe trip where polar bears may be encountered, even when a firearm is carried.

---

[1] Caldwell Outdoor Enterprises
1335 West 11th
Port Angeles, WA 98362
Phone (206) 457-3009

14. A Bold Presence

Scenario

The Coppermine River is located in a remote corner of the Northwest Territories of Canada. It is a spectacular and challenging route for experienced canoeists. There are dozens of dangerous rapids along the Coppermine. The long canyon at Rocky Defile is one of them. If your skills are good and water levels are right, Rocky Defile can be safely run. Otherwise, it's a long, cold swim to safety. Several canoeists have drowned while attempting this rapid.

Meticulous planning has gone into your Coppermine River adventure. All the major falls, rapids and portages have been carefully marked on your maps. You have noted precisely where and how past voyageurs have run, lined or portaged obstacles. Your crew has obtained as much information about the river as is humanly possible. It is your first trip to the Arctic; you want to leave nothing to chance!

When your six man crew arrives at Rocky Defile, they climb to the rim of the canyon and take a hopeful look downstream. There's a month's worth of gear in each canoe. Losing it in a capsize would be disastrous, but portaging the canyon will be a buggy all day affair. It would be wonderful if you could safely run the rapid.

From your vantage point above the river, the rapid looks manageable. Granted, there are some huge rocks and souse holes which must be avoided, but the path around them is clear. Swamping in the big waves—not hitting shallow rocks—is your major concern.

Your trip notes indicate that Rocky Defile has been successfully run by other canoeists in loaded canoes. Nonetheless, you have been pointedly advised by experts to portage around it. It's a warm sunny day; if you plan to run the rapid, now is the time to do it.

Everyone studies the drop from the canyon rim. Your partner wants to run the rapid. You—and everyone else—prefer to portage.

"Suppose we portage our gear then run the boat through empty?" Grins your friend, "Worst case scenario is that we'll have to swim."

You have an uneasy feeling but agree that the risks are minimal with an empty boat. Nonetheless, you try to convince your partner to portage, but he prods you to make the run.

"We're the best white water team here," exclaims your friend. "We can do it! Besides, it's a hot day—no biggie if we have to swim."

The Question
Should you run the rapid or portage around it?

Considerations
You have an eighteen foot Grumman canoe and no fabric splash cover. Answer these questions if you decide to run the rapid:

1. Will you run the canoe fully loaded, partially loaded, or empty?

2. You will be negotiating very big waves: Exactly where in the canoe will each paddler be situated—kneeling on the edge of his seat, bow paddler behind the center thwart, bow and stern paddlers moved closer to center, etc?

3. Are there any other precautions or final checks you wish to make before you head downstream?

Action Taken

The trip leader and his partner portaged their gear then set out to run the rapid in their empty canoe. To encourage lift in the big waves, the bow person moved back behind the bow thwart. The stern paddler kneeled at his usual location at the seat.

Just after entering the rapid, the bow paddler noted that, in the heat of excitement, he had forgotten to put on his life jacket. But it was too late; the pair were committed to the run. Seconds later, the Grumman climbed a huge wave, spun sideways in the powerful flow and capsized, spilling both paddlers into the icy water. Luckily, the stern paddler (trip leader) was thrown into an eddy near shore; his less fortunate partner—who was not wearing a life jacket—was sucked into a canoe-sized souse hole.

The stern man climbed ashore and cast a long look downstream for his friend. There was no sight of the man.

The crew spent the next day searching the rapid for signs of their friend. There was none. Ultimately, they gave up hope and paddled the remaining 200 miles to the Eskimo village of Coppermine without him. Two weeks later, an American team found the dead man's body floating in an eddy at Rocky Defile.

The Answer: In Respectful Retrospect

In the comfort of your home, it's easy to fault the trip leader for giving in to his persistent friend. Yet, things are not so simple on a strenuous wilderness canoe trip. Sure, paddling rapids is fun, but in this scenario, canoeing Rocky Defile also meant saving a long portage and avoiding the bites of black flies and mosquitoes. Enticement like this can often over-ride one's better judgment.

Moreover, the pair did take what they thought were appropriate precautions. They portaged their gear and ran their canoe empty. Good idea? Perhaps not. Consider this:

1. Their canoe was an eighteen foot Grumman—a very seaworthy craft, though one not in the league with today's high volume Royalex trippers like the Dagger Venture and Old Town Tripper. They had no fabric cover to keep out splash and no belly load to tame the ride.

2. The location of the paddlers may have been inappropriate. Level trim is the rule for rapids, regardless of how big they are. If the bow paddler moves back to lighten the bow, the stern paddler should move forward to lighten the stern. Level trim may have encouraged better control in the big waves.

3. Two fifty-pound packs tied firmly into the canoe might have increased stability in the waves and prevented the capsize. If not, the added buoyancy of the watertight packs might have floated the canoe within reach of the bow paddler. Naturally, this is all speculation.

4. Most unforgivable, of course, was that one man was not wearing his life jacket. PFD's on, lines coiled and secured on deck, and spare paddles available, are final checks that every crew should perform before running a rapid. In this case, however, the victim was thrown into a giant hole—a life jacket may not have been enough to save his life.

5. Note that the rapid was scouted from a point on the canyon rim. Waves look much flatter when viewed from above—even a few feet above! Get even with the river if you want to see the true strength of it. If you can't do that, portage, portage, portage!

6. Finally, there is the coercion factor. You should never allow a friend to convince you to do something that you fear is unsafe. As suggested in scenario #5, everyone has a river angel. Abide by her advice!

Most Coppermine River canoeists portage Rocky Defile. Those who don't usually run it in fully covered high volume Royalex canoes which are partially or fully loaded. The load increases stability in the waves and the packs—which come slightly above the gunnels—support the splash cover when the canoe takes water. A loaded canoe is less affected by whimsical currents than an empty one; it also tends to punch through waves rather than climb precariously over them. No matter—the cover keeps splash out.

Try this experiment to see the advantages of running loaded and covered versus empty and uncovered: Fill a drinking glass about one-third full of water and float it in the sink. Note how easily the glass tips over and sinks. Now, fill the glass about half full of water and cover the open end with plastic wrap. The glass is much harder to tip over.

We will never know whether a high volume Royalex canoe and splash cover, appropriate belly load, correct positioning of paddlers, and a life jacket would have prevented this drowning. Sometimes, devilish synergy springs from the wrong combination of usually benign variables. Best advice? Listen to the advice of experts and always go with your gut feeling.

15. Should I Glue

Frequently Asked Question

"I just purchased a Royalex canoe which I plan to use on rocky rivers. My buddies have told me that my canoe will last longer if I glue heavy Kevlar bang strips to the bottom of the canoe at each end. These big furry strips look plenty tough. But I think they're pretty ugly. Should I accept the bad looks and install them anyway? I also have a nice Kevlar cruising canoe that has real fine ends which chip out every time the boat hits gravel. Should I glue bang plates on it too? Please advise."

Worried in Wisconsin

The Answer

Dear Worried in Wisconsin:

I emphatically suggest that you don't glue Kevlar bang strips to your Royalex canoe. Or your Kevlar canoe. Granted, the big furry strips do absorb impact and protect the nose of your boat. But each strip weighs around two pounds when it's saturated with epoxy resin and glued to the canoe. And as you noted, they're God-awful ugly! They stick out like mole-skin on a bunion, which means they do affect the way your canoe goes through water. Take your canoes out for a spin on flat water and notice how quiet they run. Now install thick Kevlar bang plates at each end and go for another cruise. That gurgling sound you hear was not designed in by the manufacturer. It's those ugly pads which are slowing you down.

Few people know more about patching canoes than Mike Cichanowski, President of the We-no-nah Canoe Company in We-no-nah, Minnesota. We-no-nah canoes are renowned for their easy paddling characteristics and strong, lightweight construction. They're widely used by many of the best outfitters in the rocky Boundary Waters Canoe Area of Minnesota.

You won't see ugly Kevlar skid pads on the delicate ends of We-no-nah cruisers. Instead, the We-no-nah Company simply applies a narrow (inch-and-half) bead of fiberglass to each end of the canoe and tops this with a Kevlar strip of approximately equal width. The stem pieces are hardly noticeable. They weigh just a few ounces and don't affect canoe performance.

Kevlar fabric is very difficult to cut. You'll need a special (very expensive!) scissors to cut it cleanly. An ordinary scissors will tear through the fabric but the resulting cut will be a jagged mess. If you don't have Kevlar scissors you'll want to reverse the We-no-nah procedure—lay the fiberglass strip over the Kevlar strip, rather than vice versa. The glass cloth should be an inch wider and longer than the Kevlar piece.

When the epoxy is rock hard, sand the glass edges flush with the hull then spray paint the repair to match. The patch will hardly be noticeable. Note that fiberglass sands easily to a mirror finish. Kevlar cannot be sanded at all! This honey-gold fabric just frizzes into string when it's abraded.

The downside of applying fiberglass over Kevlar is that the glass will wear through quickly and expose the Kevlar beneath. A new strip of fiberglass applied over the damaged Kevlar will restore the repair.

Modern canoes are built to take a tremendous amount of abrasion and impact. Only boats that are used in serious white water or commercial outfitting probably need protective nose caps. My advice is to install bang strips when you need them and not before. Gluing Kevlar strips on a new canoe is akin to covering the leather seats of a new roadster. Cover the seats—and the nose of your canoe—when they begin to show wear. Again, most canoeists will never use their canoes hard enough to need protective stem bands.

16. Maps Don't Lie

Scenario

The Hood River begins just northeast of Takijak Lake at the edge of the Arctic Circle. From here, it flows swiftly north 180 miles through the most remote part of Canada's Northwest Territories, ultimately terminating at Bathurst Inlet on the Arctic Ocean. There are scores of tough rapids on the Hood—and many mean portages around them. It seems that on some days, portaging—and the attendant sweat and bugs—are a way of life.

Your day begins with a portage that takes two hours. There's an hour's paddle, then another long portage, followed by a short rapid you can run. At the base of the rapid is a mile long boulder field which requires you to wade, line and drag your canoe. It's a hot, sultry day and there is no escape from the dark clouds of black flies.

By six p.m. you are through the boulder field and into deep smooth water again. It's been a tough day and you're ready to camp. But, the hilly shoreline won't permit it, so you drone on in hopes of finding a suitable spot. Two hours later, you come to a huge sweeping curve, around which is a substantial falls. Another portage?

Your crew puts ashore on the inside bend and studies the map. The river widens and curves to the right for a quarter mile then it narrows and drops off as a major falls which stretches completely across the river. A contour line crosses the river near the bend; another crosses at the falls. The contour interval—or vertical distance between contour lines—is ten meters, so the drop comes in one chunk, as a 33' falls! It's clearly labeled on the map with a big fat **F**.

A hill rises ominously on river right (the inside curve). It merges into a cliff as it turns the bend. Obviously, you can't portage here. The shoreline on river left (the outside curve) is relatively flat—the place to portage. The distance to the falls on river left is around a mile. A mile long portage? Again? You re-adjust your insect head net and take a hopeful look at the cliff on the right.

"Maybe, if we stay tight against the cliff, we can paddle to the head of the falls. Could be a simple carry over," you suggest.

It's late and everyone is tired and cranky. The trip leader tosses his paddle into the canoe and says, "Dammitall, look at the map. We've got a cliff on the right and strong current all the way to the falls. Go around that bend and you won't come back! We'll pick up your bones at the base of the falls. There are no options: we've gotta ferry across and portage on the other side!"

The Question

The cliff on your right is a stopper; crossing the river and portaging on the left is the clear way to go. From your vantage point you can't see what's around the bend. Perhaps you should climb the hill and walk along the cliff to the falls for a better look. But, it's a quarter mile hike each way—twenty minutes round trip. It's eight o'clock and everyone is frazzled. The map shows your options. Should you cross the river and begin the portage or hike to the falls for a better view?

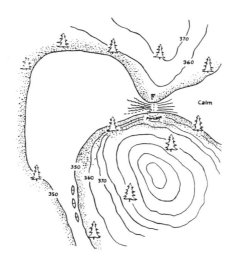

Action Taken

My partner, Marc Hebert and I were the dissenters in this group. We just couldn't face another portage. Despite considerable groans from the rest of the crew, Marc and I decided to waste time and hike to the falls. We climbed the cliff and walked the rim. It was just as Bob Dannert, our trip leader had said—the current was fast and the cliff was shear; once round the bend and there was no turning back and no way to put ashore.

"Well, Bob was right...again."

"Keep walking," said Marc.

Ten minutes later we arrived at the falls and discovered a large eddy at its head. What a deal! Just hug the right shore, ease into the eddy—which was large enough to hold a dozen boats—and take out just above the falls. The carry couldn't have been more than 100 feet!

The Answer: Moral

Maps are like history books. The story is there but the events are abridged. If you want the details of the war you'll have to do some research. Most of the planet was explored without the benefit of maps. The early explorers looked to determine what was ahead!

Rely on maps for the big picture, but trust your eyes for specific routes. Some canoeists rely too much on maps and guides. They miss the adventure of determining for themselves what's around the bend. There are many ways to skin a cat—and canoe a river.

17. Canoeing By Satellite!

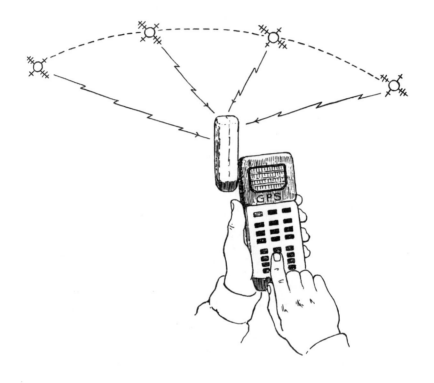

Frequently Asked Question

"I'm going to the Boundary Waters Canoe Area of Minnesota and am a bit worried about finding my way around. Some of the big lakes, like Seagull, Saganaga and Basswood look pretty confusing. I've been thinking about buying a GPS (Global Positioning System). I hear it will pinpoint your exact location anywhere on earth. Would a GPS be useful in the Boundary Waters? Can I throw away my compass if I buy one?

Lost In Space

The Answer

Dear Lost In Space:

With a GPS receiver, you can determine an accurate position anywhere on earth in a matter of minutes. Or, you can enter a set of coordinates of a place you want to go and the GPS receiver will provide a compass bearing and distance which will be updated by satellite information as you paddle. Press a button and you get a speed readout and an estimated time of arrival (ETA).

Even without a map, a GPS is extremely useful. Enter your starting position and save it as a way point. Establish other way points as you proceed, then, like Hansel and Gretel, follow your electronic bread crumbs home.

When the military discovered that GPS receivers were more accurate than they expected, they became concerned that an enemy might use a GPS to target a missile. So they introduced a random error of 15-100 meters into the civilian GPS signal. To accomplish the error, the satellites slightly delay when they send their signals.

This means that locating an obscure portage, campsite or small channel on an intricate lake is not a sure thing. A GPS will get you in the ball park but you'll need an accurate map and compass to find the ball.

Mastering the new GPS technology requires study and practice, plus a working knowledge of maps and navigational procedures. All handheld GPS units operate on small batteries, which could fail when you need them most. Consequently, it's not practical to leave a GPS on for continuous positioning. The most useful GPS feature is its ability to verify your location on a map. Also be aware that most civilian GPS models are water-repellent, not waterproof, so you don't dare use them in rain.

Maps must have some sort of reference system to which your GPS can relate. U.S. and Canadian topographic maps are marked with degrees of latitude and longitude. Canadian maps and U.S. military maps also use the Universal Trans Mercator (UTM) system which is simpler because it's decimal oriented. Any GPS can be set to read Lat/Lon or UTM coordinates, as you prefer.

Topographic maps are unpopular in the Boundary Waters because they don't show the location of campsites, portages and hiking trails. Two private companies—McKenzie and Fisher—provide specialized BWCA maps that have this important canoeing information overprinted on them. Unfortunately, neither McKenzie nor Fisher maps contain useful Lat/Lon markings or UTM coordinates, so you can't plot a GPS location. However, the McKenzie Company promises to have full Lat/Lon referencing on all their maps by 1998. The Fisher Company does not plan to add any coordinate system to their maps, so you'll need to carry a U.S.G.S. topo map for accurate positioning. Topo maps are hard to find in the Minnesota towns that service the BWCA. But you can mail order them from these sources:

For U.S Maps:
Branch of Distribution
U.S. Geological Survey
Box 25286, Federal Center
Denver, Colorado 80225

For Canadian Maps:
Canada Map Office
Dept. of Energy, Mines and Resources
615 Booth St.
Ottawa, Ontario Canada K1A OE9
1-800-465-6277

And now to your final question: "Can I throw away my compass if I buy a GPS?"

Absolutely not! Admittedly, every GPS unit provides a precise bearing and a graphic pointer that shows the way to a go to location. But the compass will provide a reading only after you have programmed in the coordinates of your objective. Programming a GPS is a tedious process, even if you have good maps. The Boundary Waters is a beautiful place—you'll want to keep your eyes on it, not your GPS! A full-frame orienteering compass provides map and ground directions at a glance and it won't quit working if you drop it or leave it out in the rain.

Satellite technology is wonderful but it's not foolproof. A good map and compass and a working brain are the tools you need most to find your way around those brawny Boundary Waters lakes.

18. Foamy Water On The Kinni

Between the awesome fury of the big rapids and the hushed quiet of meandering backwaters, there is a gentle mix of bubbling waters that challenge but do not intimidate—where pristine beauty, violet-sweet aromas and absolute solitude ravish the soul.

The Kinnikinnic River in west-central Wisconsin is such a place.

A twenty minute drive from St. Paul, Minnesota brings you to the dam and old grist mill at River Falls, Wisconsin, which marks its beginning—a reminder of when this was a working river.

The Kinni is pleasantly canoeable in spring, thoroughly walkable in summer. As one dedicated floater remarked, "You can never have too much water in this river." A week of good rain brings the Kinni to life.

It's a proud tradition among some members of the Minnesota Canoe Association to paddle their canoe on a Minnesota or Wisconsin stream at least once a month, every month of the year. This includes winter, which usually hangs around till May.

Scenario

It's a bright March morning when two Minnesota Canoe Association, instructor level canoeists off-load their Kevlar solo canoes at the base of the Kinnikinnic River dam. Significant snow is on the ground and ice clings to the shadows. The air temperature is a balmy 52°F—a perfect day for paddling.

The river is high. Very high. Water falls thickly over the dam. Usually, there's a trickle, or none at all. A foot thick film of organic foam (it looks like soap suds!) chokes the quiet pool below the dam, which marks the put-in. It's a strangely comical sight; the two canoeists have never seen the Kinni like this before.

The pair leave their gear at the landing and scout downstream. The foam continues for 100 yards, to the first bend. Who knows what lies below?

The man turns to the woman and expresses concern that "a capsize in this foam could be dangerous." She agrees and suggests they drive to the next put-in, a quarter mile downstream. The decision to canoe or cop out will have to made there. After that, it's thick forest and steep, snow-covered trails.

The view from the downstream access is more re-assuring. The foam is gone and the water runs champagne clear. But there's a small downed tree (strainer) half way across the river, and the eddys are choked with debris.

"I think we should forget it," says the man.

"Aw, c'mon; we've done this section dozens of times. Strainers and trash—big deal. We know the river and our skills. Let's do it!" says the woman.

The Question

Should you canoe the Kinni today or abort the trip? Be aware that both paddlers are highly experienced. They've done the river many times before and they are properly equipped with life jackets, extra paddles and change of clothes in a waterproof bag.

The Decision

The couple aborted the trip and spent the day hiking. That afternoon, four novice canoeists from Minneapolis put in below the dam and paddled the river without incident. They told friends they had a very good time. The next morning, another inexperienced team tried the river. As the two men were launching their canoe in the eddy below the dam, a current caught the bow and capsized the craft. One man made it to shore; the other was carried into the thick foam and drowned.

The Answer: An Abiding Philosophy

Eight people were involved in this scenario—two experienced canoeists and six beginners. Note that the experienced couple recognized the dangers of the high foam and floating debris. They drove downstream for another look, reassessed the risks and decided that the river was unsafe to paddle.

Could this experienced couple have safely negotiated the Kinni that day? Probably. But not without risk. The beginners, on the other hand, dashed obliviously downstream, unaware of the dangers. They made it on luck alone!

In scenario five I suggested that everyone has a river angel (conscience) that will point the way to safety. But river angels must be programmed with practical paddling knowledge or they won't make wise decisions. Programming means learning all you can about canoe sport. The best way is to attend paddling seminars and classes which are taught by experts. You may also want to join a canoe club:

The Minnesota Canoe Association, P.O. Box 13567, Dinkey-town Station, Minneapolis, MN 55414 is the largest and has members in all fifty states. MCA members organize canoe trips, provide paddling instruction and produce a high quality monthly magazine (HUT!).

In the off-season, canoeing texts and paddling videos are a source of tremendous knowledge and entertainment. Your public library, and every canoeing shop, has what you need to get started right.

Ever notice that the most experienced canoeists always wear their life jackets, even on quiet water on hot sunny days? Now, check out the paddle bozos who never wear them at all because they're good swimmers. Hmmm? It's a confused river angel. System file missing in her hard drive, I think.

19. Sealed With A Near Miss

The Seal River is located northeast of Tadoule Lake, in a remote corner of northern Manitoba. It is one of the most beautiful canoeing rivers in Canada, and one of the more challenging. The Seal runs fast from start to finish. The closer it gets to Hudson Bay, the faster it drops. If the water is low, the final miles to the Bay are an exciting, rock-dodging run. If the water is high, it's a heart-pounding experience, even in a splash-covered canoe!

The rapids are long and wide and often confused with hundreds of rocks. Decisions come quickly as bodies twist and paddles dance to the echoes of, "right turn, left turn, ferry left; ledge ahead—eddy in, now!" Unpredictable holes and ledges seem to appear from nowhere. Occasionally, there are falls. This story is about one of them.

Scenario

I'll take poetic license and call it Jacobson Falls, for my close observation of it placed me on intimate terms. Mistake? You be the judge. Here's what happened:

My wife, Susie and I, are in one of four canoes negotiating a wide, mile long rapid which rates a technical Class II. We are running second, about 100 feet behind my friend, Herb Hill, who is an extremely accomplished whitewater canoeist. Herb and I have shared a half dozen wild rivers. I trust his judgment and he trusts mine.

Our trip notes say there is a ledge at the base of this long rapid, and the best way around it is on river right. But the water is low and the right shore is a boulder field. It's even worse on river left. We're threading a tight zigzag course just right of center. The right bank is closest—about 200 feet away.

Suddenly, Herb turns hard left and frantically ferries up stream. He makes it into a small eddy (barely!) and stops, out-of-breath and seemingly dumbfounded as to how to proceed.

I catch it all out of the corner of my eye but I can't relate. The route ahead looks cluttered but clear.

The Question

Should I cut left now, continue on and crowd Herb's eddy, blast right into the rock garden, or run straight towards what looks like a clear vee ahead? Quick! You have three seconds to make a decision!

Action Taken

I continued straight down the tube. Seconds later, Susie screamed "falls!"

"Straighten her out!" I yelled. "At least, let's go over straight!"

Now, the canoe was in the flow, heading towards the bubbly chasm below. A Volkswagen-sized boulder suddenly appeared on my left, just six feet away.

"Back!" I screamed. And momentarily, the Dagger canoe stopped dead in its tracks. Somehow, I managed to pry the stern around and pin the boat against the rock. One more yard and we'd have gone over the falls!

Together, we pulled the heavy boat on to the huge boulder, then we looked downstream and questioned what to do.

The falls wasn't a killer, but it was a canoe breaker. We were in the proverbial predicament—safe on a rock with no place to go. I noticed that Herb had left his eddy and was edging towards shore. Everyone else was scrambling along the left bank, hip-high in water, cussing and swatting bugs as they lined and dragged their boats.

Susie and I just stood on the rock and watched. We were in no hurry—there was no place to go!

We discussed our options: Could we run the right chute? Not a chance. Ditto, the left. We could attempt an upstream ferry to Herb's eddy, but we'd never make it. Or, we could shove the canoe over the falls, then swim for it and hope for the best. Deep down, I hoped for a helicopter.

While I was deeply contemplating, Susie—who is an exploratory monkey of sorts—snaked over the huge boulder and worked her way down to the base.

"Will ya look at this," she called, in a surprisingly pleasant voice. "Nice eddy here, and a clean run-out below. Just slide her down and we're home free."

"Really?"

"Yeah!"

Two minutes later our Dagger canoe was back in the water and Susie and I were aboard and smiling. It was clear sailing to an easy eddy 100 yards downstream, where we waited an hour for our friends to finish dragging through the boulder field.

The Answer: Probable Best Course of Action

Admittedly, Susie and I took the easiest route around the falls. We didn't have to line, wade or portage. A simple lift over, that's all. But was our decision wise?

I think not. Our maneuver was unplanned and largely impossible to duplicate. Sheer power, luck and a strong downstream lean saved the day. Chances are one hundred to one we could do it again.

Moreover, I knew Herb would not suddenly turn without reason, or panic ferry just for fun. I should have heeded his cue and eddied out immediately. But, the route ahead looked clear. When I realized my mistake, it was too late—and there was only room for one boat in Herb's Eddy.

One could submit that I was following Herb too closely; but the complex nature of this rapid suggested that tight running was the best plan. However, if I were to re-do the scenario, I would probably cut to the right shore, even though there was no clear path.

Trust marks the start of this scenario. I followed Herb because I trusted him. However, trust must be tempered with the knowledge that even the best paddlers sometimes screw up. Maybe Herb just made a mistake.

The scenario ends with a saving brace and a powerful last minute ferry. For a split second, I committed to paddling over the falls. Then my vision cleared and I forced the maneuver that saved the day.

If there's a lesson here, it is that rivers have a way of rewarding determined last ditch efforts. Ever notice how one final draw often brings the canoe clear of a rock? Winston Churchill got it right when he said, "Never give up, never give up!"

20. Nose Jobs & Belly Scratches

Frequently Asked Question

I recently purchased a beautiful Kevlar canoe. I love the boat, but I don't like the dings and scratches that result from scraping rocks. Seems that no matter how careful I am, a new ding or scratch develops every time I go paddling. And whenever I hit a rock—which is pretty often on our small Missouri streams—big chunks of gel-coat chip off the bow. A friend suggested that I stick some duct tape on the bow. I tried it and it helps, but it makes the bow of the canoe look pretty tacky, especially after the tape gets scraped up. I tried a gel-coat repair kit which I got from a canoe maker but I didn't have much luck with it. The gel-coat was messy and I couldn't get the color to match. The kit was pretty expensive too—and it had a shelf life of only a year. My local power boat dealer says he can fix my canoe but it won't be cheap. I don't want to spend a fortune. Any ideas?

Madlydepressed In Missouri

The Answer

Dear Madlydepressed:

I've found that repairing chips and dings on a Kevlar or fiberglass canoe is easier if you don't follow the manufacturer's directions. But before we get specific, let's review the methods you tried:

Duct tape on the bow: Like you said, it looks tacky and it doesn't last long. Great stuff for emergencies, though. I prefer to carry duct tape in my pack, not on the outside of my canoe!

Gel-coat repair kits: Like you said, they are expensive and they have a short shelf life. However, they do a great job if you follow directions to the letter and are very patient. The book procedure calls for filling the break with color-matched liquid gel-coat, then sanding, buffing and polishing to blend the repair.

This is slow work and it's pretty frustrating. Catalyzed gel-coat is so runny that it's impossible to contain. The solution is to prop the boat at an awkward angle to level the flow, then build a well of masking tape around the resin. You can also tape plastic wrap over the resin to contain it.

When the repair hardens, you sand and buff the patch to match the hull. Getting the color to match is next to impossible unless you have a white boat or a new boat. Colors fade as canoes age. Red and blue is the worst; white and almond fade least. You'll get a perfect color match if you simply polish out the hardened patch and spray it with auto acrylic that matches the color of your boat.

My wife and I use our three Kevlar canoes hard, and one or more of them is always in need of repair. Unless there's structural damage, I usually make repairs once a year, in the fall, so all will be right come spring. The bow stem of my wife's 1974 Mad River LadySlipper has been repaired at least twenty times. It still looks like new. Here's how I fix the serious dings.

Materials Needed

- White polyester putty (available at marinas) or gray auto body putty. Or, mix epoxy resin (make a paste) with glass micro-spheres or micro-balloons. See the footnote at the end of this section.

- Sixty and 100 grit dry sandpaper, and 200 grit wet-dry finishing paper.

- A spray can of matching auto acrylic.

- Fiberglass boat wax (it contains a mild abrasive). Or, auto paste wax and pumice.

Procedure

1. Pick out the shards of damaged gel coat with the blade of a knife.

2. Catalyze the polyester putty (use extra MEKP to produce a hot mix) and work it into the break to over-flowing. The putty is thick and won't run so there's no need to build a tape well.

3. When the putty is firm (about ten minutes), slice off the excess with a knife. Allow the remainder to cure completely (another half hour), then sand it level with progressive grits of sandpaper. Finish to silky smoothness with 400 grit sandpaper.

4. Spray paint the patch. When the paint has dried, blend the paint to match the hull with a mixture of paste wax and pumice. Or, use fiberglass boat wax, which contains pumice.

That's all there is to it. Down time on the canoe is less than an hour. And you'll have a perfect color match.

If you have a natural gold Kevlar canoe, you'll discover that it's almost impossible to get a perfect color match when you make repairs to the ends. One solution is to repair the gel-coat damage as described above, then mask a short, artificial water-line along the bow and stern (figure 20). Paint the masked area an attractive color. Dark brown looks elegant and unobtrusive.

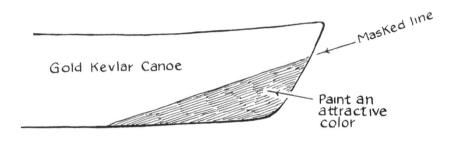

Scratches

Show me a canoe that hasn't been scratched and I'll show you a canoe that hasn't been used! Gel-coat is a fraction of a millimeter thick; it's there for appearance not strength. Scratches—even deep ones—don't affect the integrity or performance of a canoe.

Shallow scratches can often be polished out with auto buffing compounds. Some of the more aggressive automotive paste cleaners do a fair job, especially when they're applied by machine. Use a light touch on the buffer. Bear down hard and you may cut into the Kevlar below!

Deep scratches are best left alone, unless they are so deep that they abrade the Kevlar beneath. If gold furry stuff (damaged Kevlar) protrudes from the scratch, you'll want to make repairs. If the damage is light, simply flow epoxy resin[1] into the cut. When it has hardened, polish it out and paint it.

Heavily scored or broken Kevlar should be covered with a fiberglass patch. Blend the edges of the hardened patch to the surrounding hull then paint it. Be sure to use fiberglass, not Kevlar, for cosmetic patches. Kevlar cannot be sanded!

---

[1] I prefer West System® epoxy, which is formulated for boat building and repair. It is available by mail from the GOUGEON BROTHERS, INC., POB 908, Bay City, MI 48707. Phone (517) 684-7286. Gougeon, Inc. has everything you need to repair your canoe. Ask for their catalog.

21. Thinking Straight

Frequently Asked Question

I want to buy a new canoe paddle and am considering one with a bent shaft. I know that bent paddles are the clear choice for racing, but I hear they're awkward in rapids. The rivers up here are a mix of flat water and whitewater, so I must have a paddle that works well in both situations. I have a big seventeen-foot Royalex tripping canoe. It's seaworthy and reliable, but not sporty or fast. Should I buy a bent shaft or stay straight?

Bentley Whitewatertripper
Caribou Jaw, Saskatchewan

The Answer

Dear Bentley Whitewatertripper:

Bent shaft paddles are advantageous in almost any canoe—even a whitewater tripper. I carry two paddles on my wilderness trips—a straight 56-inch whitewater paddle made by the Grey Owl Company in Canada, and a 54-inch, twelve-degree bent-shaft Zaveral[1]. I use the synthetic Zaveral almost exclusively in my seventeen-foot Dagger Venture canoe. I switch to the wooden Grey Owl in rapids.

Here are some things to consider when selecting a bent shaft paddle:

1. Your bent-shaft paddle should be about two inches shorter than your favorite straight paddle.

2. You'll need a longer paddle in a high-seated tripping canoe than in a low-seated racer or cruiser. Fifty to fifty-two inches is a good length for a bent-shaft paddle that will be used in a shallow racing or cruising canoe; fifty-four to fifty-six inches is better for a deep tripper.

3. There are five, twelve, fourteen and fifteen degree bends. Until recently, racers preferred 14-degree bends. Now, they're hot on 12-degree bends, possibly because the slightly straighter shaft allows a more upright position and a smoother flow of power.

4. Two things to look for in a bent paddle:

(A) Both sides of the paddle face should look the same. Avoid models that have a flat power face and a back face that has substantial camber or a thick spline. Symmetrical blades are more forgiving and pleasant to use than asymmetrical ones.

(B) Lightweight racing and cruising canoes are like sports cars—a few strokes get them to full speed. Stiff paddles may be advantageous as they don't bend and absorb energy when power is applied. But heavily loaded tripping canoes are more like locomotives—they must be pushed up to speed. Hence, the paddles used should have some flex to absorb shock. Tennis elbow (paddler's elbow?) may be partly due to sustained use of a paddle that is too stiff. Note that state-of-the-art carbon fiber paddles have no flex at all. For this reason, hybrid (carbon-fiber/fiber-glass) paddles—like the wonderful Black Rec Zaverals, may be the best choice for use in heavy canoes.

Of course, there are some wonderful wooden bent-shaft paddles. Try to find one that weighs less than eighteen ounces.

Running rapids with a bent paddle: Many accomplished canoeists prefer to use bent shaft paddles for everything, even running rapids. It's simply a matter of getting used to the paddle and adapting to its limitations. For example, draws and (especially) crossdraws are more effective with an angled blade than a straight one. And steering—a la the pitch or J-stroke—is easier because the blade runs closer to the keel line. On the other hand, high and low braces are awkward. The straight shaft is the right tool in rapids; the bent-shaft is best every place else.

To summarize: your bent paddle should be about two inches shorter than your favorite whitewater paddle; both paddle faces should be symmetrical, and there should be some flex in the shaft. A twelve degree bend is best over the long haul.

---

[1] Grey Owl Paddles, Inc. 62 Cowansview Rd. Cambridge, Ontario, Canada NiR 7N3. Phone (519) 622-0001

Zaveral Racing Equipment, RD 1, Box 150, Mt. Upton, NY 13809. Phone (607) 563-2487

---

22. Three Timely Decisions

Newcomers to canoeing secretly express the fear that they will drown in a rapid or inadvertently paddle over a falls. These concerns are real but they're secondary to the omnipresent dangers of crossing open water in bad weather. Scenario #12 drives home the point.

Each of the following scenarios asks the same question: "Should we stay put where it's safe, or travel on?" Of course, the safe choice is to hang around until the weather improves. But when the textbook closes, there are concerns and frustrations which must be addressed. Here are some of them:

- "Our charter float plane comes tomorrow. If we're not where we're supposed to be, when we're supposed to be, we'll miss our flight. Of course he'll come again in a day or three—but, he'll charge us for another run!"

- "I must be home tomorrow. If I miss work, I'm dead!"

- "We've been sitting on this rock, staring at the waves for hours. It's getting dark and there's no place to camp. We gotta go!"

- "We planned 'one day in five' as down time for wind. It's only our fourth day and we've been here for three of 'em! Everyone is going nuts. Looks to me like the lake is settling down. Let's move!"

Scenario #1: On The Ocean

The North Knife River flows into Hudson Bay, about thirty miles north of Churchill, Manitoba. Canoeists who do the North Knife have three options:

1) Arrange for a power boat from Churchill to pick you up at the mouth of the river. This is the safest alternative but the boat won't come if the weather is bad.

2) Arrange for a float plane pick-up at Dymond Lake Lodge, which is located at the edge of a small tundra lake (Dymond Lake), six miles south of the Knife River, on Hudson Bay. Hudson Bay is cold, shallow and rocky, and there may be polar bears about. Add wind—which threatens to blow you aground—and it's an adrenaline-pumping ride. You must travel at high tide, which comes just twice a day. Exposed rocks make it difficult to travel close to shore. Often, you'll be a quarter mile out! In good weather, you can paddle to the lodge in about two hours.

3) Paddle to Churchill. Dozens of canoeists have done it. Some have drowned trying! Most who have made the trip say they would never do it again. You must come into Churchill on an incoming tide or you won't get in!

My crew chose option (2).

We arrived at the Bay the night before our scheduled flight. The wind was blowing bloody murder and the waves were twice as high as my Chevy van. Canoeing the Bay was out-of-the-question. Our float plane was scheduled to pick us up at Dymond Lake at 0800 the following morning. We'd have to leave by six or we'd never make it.

At midnight the wind was still howling. I woke up at two a.m. and there was no change. I was sure we'd miss our plane—and the train to Thompson, which runs once a day, every other day. A one-day delay would cost each person two days of lost time, plus another $300 for the plane ride, motel and meals in Churchill.

A friend awakens me at 4 a.m. and suggests I "take a look." The wind is down considerably, though there are still small white caps far out on the Bay. High tide comes in thirty minutes. Would you stay put or make a run for it?

Scenario #2: Crossing Wollaston Lake

The Fond du Lac River is one of the nicest routes in Saskatche-wan. But, getting there requires perseverance. Most canoeists drive the ominous tote road (200 miles) from LaRonge, to Points North. Here, they charter a float plane and fly into the Fond du Lac system. It's expensive, of course, so budget-minded paddlers usually access the river by way of Reindeer and Wollaston lakes. Sigurd Olson's wonderful book, Runes of the North describes his adventures on these lakes.

The two young Americans began their canoe trip at Wollaston Lake, about thirty miles south of the Fond du Lac River. A strong headwind produced huge white caps, so they decided to play it safe and follow the west shore of the lake to the mouth of the river. Two days later they had completed ten miles and had twenty to go. They were wearing themselves out and making no time at all. At this rate, their vacation would be over before they reached the Fond du Lac. They outlined their options:

1) Continue along the west shore, hopping from bay to bay. Better to make five safe miles a day then to make none!

2) Go at night when the wind was slightly down. They could run a bee line from bay to bay. This would be more dangerous than following the shore but it would save a lot of time.

3) Find a good campsite and hang around till the wind stops. Surely, it must stop eventually! When it does, try to make up for lost time.

Choose an option and support your decision.

Scenario #3: The Black Lake Crossing

Fond du Lac River canoeists may end their trip with a float plane pick-up at Black Lake, or paddle across Black Lake (it takes nearly a day) to the small community of Stony Rapids. From here, they can return to LaRonge on a wheeled airplane—a scheduled DC-3 or Hawker. This is much less expensive than chartering a float plane.

However, getting to Stony Rapids can be difficult if the wind is up—which is usually one day in two. Black Lake is very shallow and wide and it has only one island for cover. Even a moderate wind produces ominous waves which stop large power boats. An 18 or 20-foot aluminum boat, with two motors is the craft of choice for fishing Black Lake.

Six Americans are preparing to canoe across Black Lake. They are scheduled to fly out of Stony Rapids at five p.m. the following day. It's supper time and storming. Only a fool would go out on the lake right now.

The crew decides to make camp and go when the wind dies down. Midnight comes and the wind is still blowing strong. The leader peers through the tent screen and sees whitecaps. He says, "forget it" and goes back to sleep. At one o'clock, everyone arises for another look. Now, only small whitecaps remain. Right now the lake looks safe to paddle. It may not be when the sun comes up! The crew begins to argue. It's a split vote. Should they run for it or delay a day and miss their plane.

Action Taken—#1: On The Ocean

Binoculars revealed a few white caps far out to sea, but there were none within unaided sight of land. I gave the order to "secure splash covers and go!" A dazzling sunrise and a flurry of ripples hypnotically guided us around our protected point and into the teeth of Hudson Bay. Riffles turned to waves which blended to huge rollers. Up one, down another, and a pushy tail wind all the way. It was an exhilarating ride to Dymond Lake Lodge, but we were in control all the way.

We arrived at the lodge at 7:50. Our Cessna touched down fifteen minutes later. The pilot said he knew we'd be there. The day continued to improve, and by noon the Bay was smooth as the bottom of my canoe.

If we had waited we would have missed our plane and high tide. It was go now or wait twelve hours. I'd play this scene the same way again. The fact that the decision was made quickly, saved the day. An hour's delay would have put us on the next day's calendar.

Action Taken—#2: Crossing Wollaston Lake

The two young men chose option #2. They decided to save time by cutting across the smaller bays. They lost control of their canoe on a wave and capsized in the icy water. One man drowned; the other made it to shore where he was picked up by fishermen several days later.

Conversations with the survivor suggested that he and his friend knew they were making a mistake by cutting across bays. The men said they were frustrated because they were wasting precious vacation time.

Mother nature always wins! I'd have found a nice campsite, put on the tea pot and waited till the weather cleared. Wollaston can be crossed in less than a day if the wind is right. Better to stay put, wait for a safe window, then "put the ash to 'er."

Action Taken—#3: Crossing Black Lake

After several minutes of arguing, one crew member turned to the leader and said, "You're the leader, Bill," make a decision!

He did. The crossing took five hours. Ten minutes after they reached the far shore, the wind came up again.

Moral? Every canoe trip needs a leader who has the final say. In scenarios #1 and #3, timing was critical. In the first case, a late start would have cost the crew a good deal of money and lost time, without significantly reducing the risk. In #3, a ten minute delay would have been dangerous!

Rule by committee may be the fair way to run a wilderness canoe trip, but it is not necessarily the best way!

23. Illinois Trained & Canada Bound

Frequqently Asked Question

Some friends and I are planning a canoe trip on a river in Northern Canada and are concerned that our skills may not be up to the challenge. We all do a lot of paddling here in Illinois and we've been to the Boundary Waters several times. Our southern Illinois rivers don't have big rapids like those we'll encounter in Canada. Our biggest lakes are a few miles long and are dam controlled. Can we adequately prepare for our dream trip here in Illinois? Or, must we go north for more training? Are there techniques we should master? Instruction we should obtain? Books and pamphlets we should read? Please advise.

Rapidlydreaming Aboutcanada

The Answer

Dear Rapidlydreaming:

It's tough to prepare for a big Canadian river in Illinois. Rapids on the premier Canadian routes are longer, wider and much more powerful than any in the midwest. Even the largest lakes in the Boundary Waters (like Basswood and Saganaga) are small potatoes compared to the little ones in Canada. And you're a long way from help, which means you may not get a second chance if you mess up.

Canoeing wilderness rivers should be an apprenticeship process during which skills are slowly and thoughtfully developed. It takes time—and some hair-raising experiences—to develop the proper respect for a wild river. Don't rush it by doing something stupid!

Begin the learning curve by reading everything you can find about canoeing wild rivers. The most recommended texts are Bill Mason's *Path of the Paddle* and my books, *Canoeing Wild Rivers*, and *Canoeing & Camping, Beyond the Basics*. Be sure to see (study them!) Bill Mason's wonderful *Path of the Paddle* videos. *Whitewater Doubles* is the most valuable in the series. Most canoe shops and some public libraries have it.

Reading lists that include the diaries of past voyageurs who've canoed the rivers of your interest, are available free from some Canadian provinces. The Northwest Territories has the most complete list.

Chicagoland Canoe Base, 4019, Narragansett, Ave., Chicago, IL 60634. Phone (312) 777-1489, is your most complete source of new and old canoeing books. If Chicagoland doesn't have it, nobody does!

Northern Books, PO Box 211, Station P, Toronto, Ontario Canada M5S 2S7, is a good source of used, rare and select new books on historical and modern Canadian canoeing. Northern Books is the brain child of George Luste, one of Canada's most respected wilderness canoeists.

Wilderness Collection, 716 Delaware Ct. Lawton, MI 49065 (616) 624-4410, also has an inventory of historical canoeing books.

You'll want to subscribe to *CHE-MUN, Nastawgan, KANAWA, Canoe & Kayak*, and *Paddler* magazines.

CHE-MUN (The Journal of Canadian Wilderness Canoeing) was founded in 1973 by Nick Nickels. It's now in the hands of Michael Peake, a renown Canadian explorer. *CHE-MUN* emphasizes serious canoe adventures. Address: *CHE-MUN*, Box 548, Station O, Toronto, Ontario, Canada M4A 2P1.

NASTAWGAN, is the quarterly Journal of the Wilderness Canoe Association. It's similar to *CHE-MUN* but less expedition oriented. Address: Wilderness Canoe Association, P.O. Box 48022 Davisville Postal Outlet, 1881 Yonge St., Toronto, Ontario, Canada M4S 3C6.

KANAWA is the official publication of the Canadian Recreational Canoe Association. For subscriptions call, (519)473-2109 or (519)641-1261. Better yet, join the CRCA and get the magazine free. You'll also get a nice decal for your car and a classy pin for your hat, plus a book list and product information. Address: 1029 Hyde Rd., Suite 5, Hyde Park, Ontario, Canada N0M 1Z0.

Canoe & Kayak (P.O. Box 3146, Kirkland, WA 98083-3146) and Paddler (P.O. Box 1341, Eagle, ID 83616) are the only U.S. canoeing magazines.

So much for homework. Now, on to honing skills. You should be comfortable in Class II-III whitewater before the wheels roll north. Your local canoe shop can suggest a paddling school that will provide the instruction you need. Be sure you tell the school that you want to learn the techniques of wilderness canoeing, not white-water slalom! Whitewater canoes handle like sports cars; tripping canoes perform like sixteen wheelers. When there's trouble ahead, whitewater boats spin bow upstream and race to a safe eddy. Tripping canoes turn sluggishly and backferry!

The rule in Canada is, if you can't run the rapid, line around it. If you can't line, portage! You've been to the Boundary Waters so you already know about portaging. Lining heavily loaded canoes down complex rapids is, however, another matter. You can learn the basics on the small rivers near your home, but you'll need some mean class III water to complete your education. On some Canadian routes you may encounter dangerous rapids which can't be run and can't be portaged because the shore line is massed with boulders or choked with vegetation. Then, you'll have to line—and you'd better know what you're doing!

Newcomers are often amazed at the size and power of northern waters. Some rapids stretch for miles and are hundreds of feet wide! Often, you have to decide in advance whether to follow the right or left side of a wide river. It may be difficult or impossible to cross over if you make the wrong choice. Few rivers in the U.S.A. compare in size with the big water you'll find in northern Canada. Down home streams are not adequate training for what you'll encounter up north!

I've found that the best way to develop big water skills is to take things slowly, one step at a time. For example, do the Boundary Waters a few times, then move north to some easy Ontario rivers, like the English, Turtle and Steel. Then, it's on to more challenging Ontario waters, like the Kopka, Missinaibi and Winisk. Now, you're ready for the Fond du Lac and Clearwater in Saskatche-wan, then the Knife and Seal in Manitoba. After that, it's the Northwest Territories and routes above the tree line. Only the very best canoeists should paddle Arctic rivers. It would be irresponsible to suggest otherwise.

If you want to shorten the learning curve, make your first Canadian adventure with an expert who knows the ropes. Fully outfitted and guided canoe trips are often advertised in the pages of canoeing magazines. I can vouch for the quality of trips sponsored by the Science Museum of Minnesota, St. Paul, The University of Minnesota, Duluth (UMD), and The Northwest Passage, a Wilmette, Illinois company. Black Feather is probably the best known tripping company in Canada.

Meanwhile, seek challenges at home. Paddle in all kinds of weather, especially bad weather. Get out and paddle those dam controlled waters when the wind is up and the power boats have high-tailed it to shore. Seek out and ride speed boat wakes on a sunny Sunday when the reservoir is packed with hot-rodders. Paddle early in the spring, late in the fall, and in the dead of winter. You can never learn too much about canoeing!

24. A Speedy Demise

Scenario

You and three friends are planning to canoe the Kopka River in northern Ontario. This breathtakingly beautiful route consists largely of small and medium sized lakes and gentle current, but it also includes a number of short, challenging rapids. Five major falls which you must portage around, round out the trip. The portages aren't marked and their locations aren't always obvious. Two portages are particularly noteworthy. One requires you to lower canoes and gear by mountaineering rope 100 feet down a canyon wall! Another follows an old stream bed which is choked with hip-high boulders which you must jump across. This portage is extremely dangerous, especially if you have short legs, poor balance and a heavy canoe. A reasonably good trip guide, which shows the location of portages and rapids is available free from the Ontario Ministry of Natural Resources. You plan to write for it immediately!

To summarize, the Kopka consists of mostly small and medium sized lakes and gentle current, with some short, challenging rapids and a few tough portages. Some portages are hard to find, but that's part of the challenge of canoeing a wild river.

Your friends own a 17' Grumman canoe which weighs 75 pounds. You have an 18' We-no-nah Jensen which weighs twenty pounds less. That's a real difference on the portages! More important, the Jensen is much faster and easier to paddle than the portly Grumman. However, it's less seaworthy and it turns reluctantly in rapids. On the other hand, the runnable rapids on the Kopka are short and well defined. You can easily portage or line any rapid that you feel is too tough for the Jensen.

The Question

You and your partner are accomplished paddlers with an affinity for long, lean canoes. Should you bring the sleek Jensen or rent a heavier, higher volume canoe? Read the Kopka background again, then decide.

Action Taken

The men chose to bring the Jensen, which kept them in the lead nearly all the time. On the fifth day of their trip, they powered around the bend that marked the start of a strong rapid (it was on the map), missed the obscure portage, and entered the slick water above the first drop. When they realized they had gone too far, they eddied out of the main current and turned around, intent on paddling back upstream to calm water. But the deep, fine ends of the Jensen caught the eddy line, and the craft capsized, spilling both men into the frigid water.

The bow man hung onto a pack as long as his cold-numbed hands would allow, then he succumbed to the power of the rapid and was carried downstream to the bitter end. The rapid—which was filled with boulders and strainers—would probably rate Class IV, if it were runnable!

Meanwhile, the man's partner held on to the canoe till it broke up in the rocks, then he pulled himself out of the water into an eddy and attempted to find his way through the woods to the portage, which came out in a quiet bay near the rapid.

Unaware their friends were in trouble, the men in the Grumman started the portage. They completed the carry without seeing either of their companions, then they continued the trip, believing their friends were still in the lead.

The rest of the story involves dangerous bouts with hypothermia and the near death of the man who swam the rapid. How all four got down river and over the awful portages is another tale. You can read the full account in my book, *Campsite Memories*. It's called the "Story of the Blue Canoe."

The Answer: In Retrospect

The first mistake was made before the wheels rolled north. The 18' Jensen is wonderful for cruising benign waters but it is not, by any account, suitable for rapids—any rapids! One could argue that the men should not have missed the portage. But human error is a reality of wilderness travel. Everyone makes mistakes. The question is, will your gear allow you to recover from them? The men were both good paddlers; they probably could have eddied upstream if they had been paddling a tripping canoe instead of a flatwater rocket that wouldn't turn. The Jensen was the simply the wrong boat for the trip. Period!

The rule in the wilderness is to choose a canoe that is up to the challenge of the worst reasonable scenario you can expect to experience. Eddying out in the midst of a strong rapid is reasonable, and so is hitting rocks and capsizing. This rules out sleek, fast canoes that turn reluctantly, low volume ones that sink in waves, and fragile craft that are easily holed by rocks. On the other hand, pure-bred whitewater canoes have no place in the wilds either. They're too slow and hard to keep on course in wind and they may have not have enough room to carry the gear you need. Wilderness tripping canoes aren't much fun to paddle, but they are versatile, trustworthy and reliable.

Many years ago, a very accomplished solo canoeist paddled Ontario's Missinaibi River in a Pat Moore designed Proem canoe. The Proem is a very small (12') tippy canoe. It has a lot of volume for its size, but its highly asymmetric shape and rounded bottom have earned it the title of drowning machine. Only the very best paddlers can stay upright in a Proem, let alone paddle one well. This boat is fine for messing around on quiet water, but it's out-of-place on a wilderness river.

Given this glowing testimony, why would anyone choose such a boat for a trip on a tough Canadian river? More importantly, why would he photograph his trip then show the slides to a novice audience? Ego, perhaps? Stupidity? Or, to show off his skills? I saw the man's presentation and shook my head in disgust. I hope the audience didn't believe a word he said!

The final word in the Kopka River scenario is that the teams should have stayed together on the river. Eight eyes are better than four, especially when portages are hard to find. It's that old devil, ego, again. He has no place on a wilderness canoe trip!

25. Unfounded Fears

Frequently Asked Question

Some friends and I are planning to canoe a remote river in northern Canada. We've paddled a lot of local rivers here in Michigan, and we've been to the Boundary Waters several times. We haven't had any formal canoe training, but we read a lot and paddle a lot. And we're not hot dogs! We respect the river and don't take chances. I think we're ready to make our first big trip.

Nonetheless, I have a deep fear that we'll screw up and paddle over a falls or drown in a rapid. I've studied my maps and marked every danger. If there's any doubt, we'll line or portage. But I'm still worried that I might die on this canoe trip. In fact, I'm thinking of increasing my life insurance in case I don't come back. I don't mean to sound pessimistic, because I'm really very optimistic and excited about doing this trip. But deep down, I'm afraid to go. Is this normal?

Fearful Fran

The Answer

Dear Fearful:

Rest easy; the fear (let's call it concern) you express is perfectly normal. And healthy. It shows that beneath your tough outward appearance there's a warmly beating heart. Rest assured that you are not alone! Every wilderness canoeist I know secretly admits some trepidation that his or her skills are inadequate to meet the challenge.

Note that it's the experienced canoeists who worry most. Beginners seldom give the matter much thought. Why? Because it takes a fair amount of field experience to appreciate the dangers of a wild river, let alone learn what they are. How can you relate to the danger of swamping far from shore on a big lake, capsizing in ice cold water, or being caught in a strainer, if you've never done it or seen it?

Mild controllable fear is nature's way of telling you to slow down and think before you act. At the other extreme is foolhardiness, and every whitewater club has members that qualify. I hope that none of your paddling friends are so inclined.

Dr. Bill Forgey, nationally known outdoorsman and author sums it up:

> Somehow on long trips, the uncertainty of the next day's travel, the food supply, the amount of time, all seem to gnaw at me— perhaps in many ways spoiling the trip. Why do I take these things so seriously? Perhaps I'm not cut out for wilderness travel. I asked Sigurd Olson one day about this. He laughed and said that he'd asked the same question to the noted Canadian explorer, Charles Camsell at the Explorer's Club one day. Camsell replied that he'd spent most of his adult life exploring the bush and had been scared during nine-tenths of it.

Some whitewater canoeists have a unique method of rating rapids. There are one pee, two pee and three pee rapids. One pee rates about Class II on the international scale; three pee earns a V or VI! On some western U.S. rivers, the stench of urine above difficult rapids is so strong that authorities have posted signs asking people to do it in the water, not on land.

Again, your feelings are perfectly normal. I'm certain that you will not paddle over a falls or drown in a rapid this summer. Why? Because you are a skilled paddler, you've done your homework and you know your limitations. Most important, you respect the river and know that you can't beat nature at her own game.

Have fun in Canada this summer. Spend your extra dollars on souvenirs, not life insurance. You'll find good deals on beautiful native artwork in the northern communities.

26. Two Is Company

Frequently Asked Question

Something came up and my partner just dropped out of our canoe trip plans. Now, there's an odd number of people. No one wants to ride dead weight, and I question the safety of three in a canoe. We'll be canoeing in Quetico Park in Ontario. It's mostly lakes but I think there are some rapids we can run.

No one is willing to quit the trip, and we can't seem to find another warm body. We'll probably have to go with three in one canoe. Are there concerns we should address?

Deadweight Donna

The Answer

Dear DD:

Three to a canoe is common practice in lake country and on gentle rivers. In fact, it's Standard Operating Procedure in most Minnesota tripping camps which service the Boundary Waters Canoe Area. These two things will add to the comfort and safety of your passenger.

1.   Provide a sit upon—a boat cushion or thick closed-cell foam sitting pad for the duffer. A thick boat cushion is best because it keeps buttocks dry when the canoe takes water. This is especially important when you make long lake crossings on cold, windy days.

2.   Make a removable carrying yoke for the canoe. A simple clamp device works best. My book, Canoeing & Camping, Beyond The Basics illustrates a proven pattern.

Remove the yoke to provide unobstructed room for the passenger and easier loading of packs. Clamp the yoke in place when it's time to portage. We generally travel with three packs to a canoe in two person boats, and two packs to a canoe in three person boats. One pack sits upright against the rear thwart to provide a backrest for the duffer. The other pack rides behind the bow seat for balance. This arrangement provides room for the passenger to stretch out. The uncluttered mid-section (no confining yoke) is also a safety advantage in the event of a capsize.

It's never safe to run rapids with three in a canoe. Two hundred pounds of potatoes is a more stable and predictable load than half that weight of human cargo. Of course, you can safely run riffles and wide open Class I-II drops. Bigger stuff is best lined or portaged.

Be aware that a removable yoke is not as strong as one that's bolted in place. The structural integrity of a canoe depends largely on the strength and security of its center thwart. Yokes that secure with clamps may pop out in a rough water capsize and allow the canoe to wrap—another reason why you should not run rapids with three to a canoe.

My own preference would to be to provide a solo canoe for the extra person. Now, we're talking real fun! If you haven't paddled a pure-bred solo canoe on a wilderness trip, you're in for a treat. These little boats are as fast and capable as big ones, if they're piloted well. Tip: don't let your friends try your solo canoe unless you're willing to give it up for the rest of the trip!

I would never paddle a wild Canadian river with three to a canoe, even a big canoe. Remember, the variable here is a an unpredictable shifting load, not an over-load!

27. What's Wrong Here?

Scenario

The Rum River in east-central Minnesota is, by all accounts, a typical home town stream. It twists lazily along, like a garden snake on a hot afternoon. There are some riffles but no real rapids. Occasionally, a downed tree requires a lift-over or carry around. Otherwise, there are no real portages. In summer, kids float the Rum in inner tubes. In spring, fishing's the thing.

Every community has a Rum River which is the recreational life blood of the town. Most are smooth and quiet streams which are not considered dangerous. But when the snows of winter become spring run-off, the usually quiet snake develops fangs. Then suddenly, local residents are horrified to learn there's been a close call or a drowning on their home town river!

It was a cold, rainy day in April, 1972, just after snow melt. The Rum raced with winter's run-off and was flooded high above her banks. The manicured lawns were gone and many of the homes and roads were under water. A newly erected sign by the put-in read: **DANGER, HIGH WATER**!

Four friends came to canoe the river that day. Two of them lost their canoe and nearly, their lives. The couple that capsized made many mistakes. They're listed below, along with things they did right and wrong, and things that didn't matter. See if you can tell which is which. Make three lists—GOOD , BAD, and DIDN'T MATTER—then place each statement into the correct category. Some errors are obvious; others require an in-depth knowledge of canoesport.

Check your answers when you're done, then read *WHAT HAPPENED!*

What They Did
Categorize each statement as
'GOOD' or 'BAD' or 'OF NO CONSEQUENCE'

1. Canoed the Rum when it was in flood stage.
2. Disregarded the **DANGER** sign at the put-in.
3. The man and woman both wore Stearn's *Gatsby* panel-style life jackets, not the yellow kapok filled kind that is popular in summer camps.
4. They secured the safety chain at the bottom of their life jackets.
5. The couple had a well-trained sixty-pound dog in their canoe.
6. The man wore his car keys on a parachute cord around his neck.
7. The man had a Swiss army knife in his pocket.
8. The man wore cotton-waffle long underwear, a wool shirt and blue jeans.
9. The woman wore polypropylene long underwear, a thick acrylic sweater and polyester stretch pants.
10. The woman wore a two-piece rain-suit.
11. The man wore a military style poncho to protect him from rain.
12. Ten feet of rope was attached to each end of the canoe.
13. The rope was wound around the seats and tied off so it would be secure in a capsize.
14. They had a change of clothes in a waterproof bag, inside a nylon pack-sack.
15. They secured the packsack to a thwart (buckled a shoulder strap around it) so it wouldn't be lost if they capsized.
16. They had one spare paddle.
17. The paddle was left loose in the canoe—it was not tied to thwarts.
18. They had a compass and a special *canoe map* of the river.
19. They had not paddled the river before.
20. They did not know how to ferry a canoe across a strong current.

The Answers
Good

3. It's easier to swim while wearing a trim, panel-style life jacket, than a bulky kapok model. Tubular style PFD's—like those worn by whitewater canoeists—are the best life jackets of all.

7. A knife is essential on a canoe trip. However, a folding knife should be secured to a lanyard so it won't be lost. The best river knives have fixed blades or are folders that can be opened with one hand.

9. The woman was well-dressed for 1972. She understood the dangers of hypothermia.

10. A two-piece rain-suit is much safer than a poncho or knee-length rain shirt. Try swimming while wearing a poncho and you'll see why!

12. Rope or grab loops are essential safety equipment on a river canoe.

14. A change of clothes is standard on every canoe trip, even one that lasts only a few hours.

16. One spare paddle is minimal; two is better.

18. Good planning! Bring a map and compass on every canoe trip.

Bad

1. Even highly skilled paddlers won't canoe a river that's in flood stage!

2. Most signs don't address the concerns of canoeists. This one happened to be right on target!

4. Safety chains are for quiet water only. They lightly secure a life jacket that is not zipped up. Never use a safety chain in conjunction with a zipped-up life vest. You may not be able to remove the jacket in an emergency if the chain is secured. Safety chains are unsafe—the reason why they are no longer used on life jackets!

5. Dogs are wonderful, especially well-trained ones. But not in rapids or on a flooded river!

6. Never wear anything on a cord around your neck. This mistake nearly cost the man his life!

8. The man was not properly dressed for the weather. He should have consulted his wife.
11. See #10 in the Good section.
13. The rope was tied off, and therefore, useless for rescue work. It should have been coiled and secured under a tight loop of shock-cord on deck.
20. The forward and backferry are the most important techniques in river canoeing. Ferries enable you to maneuver laterally across a current, without sliding downstream, into an obstacle. Use the backferry to avoid falls, dams and rocks that are too close to paddle around. Use the forward ferry to cross a wide river, or to hop from eddy to eddy. You are not ready for the river until you can confidently ferry your canoe. If ducks can do it, you can too!

Of No Consequence

15. It takes time to unbuckle a pack strap. For this reason, it's best to secure things with clips, FASTEX® buckles or carabiners. Number 15 plays no part in the scenario.
17. Some whitewater experts lightly secure their spare paddle; others don't bother. Either way, it's not important here.
19. Naturally, it's an advantage to have paddled a river before. But these folks had a special *canoe map.* High water aside, they knew what to expect!

What Happened?

The canoes had to pass between the pilings of a bridge which was located about fifty yards below the put-in. This required that the paddlers ferry out from shore, then turn downstream and run between the pilings.

The first canoe did it right and easily cleared the pilings. The second canoe didn't know how to ferry. They paddled straight out and broadsided the bridge. They tried to lean downstream but the dog jumped out upstream and capsized the canoe. The woman was swept into the branches of a downed tree (strainer). She climbed on to the tree but couldn't get ashore.

In a freak accident, the cord around the man's neck caught on a yoke pad when the canoe capsized. He nearly strangled on the spot! The man reached for his Swiss army knife with hopes of cutting himself free, but the knife was gone. He later told rescuers "I probably couldn't have got it open anyway." Seconds later, the fiberglass canoe broke in half and the man was whisked downstream and into the same tree as his wife. As the man struggled on to the log, a branch caught his life jacket and pulled him under. He unzipped the life jacket but couldn't get free of it because the safety chain was attached. One second the man was up for air; the next he was underwater. This continued for half a minute, until he was free of the life jacket.

Fortunately, the paddlers in the other canoe were on the scene. They borrowed a rope from a nearby home and rescued the man and his wife. As they pulled the couple ashore, they noticed that two canoes were trapped in the strainer. Evidently, four other people had tried to canoe the Rum that day!

In case you're wondering, the dog got out okay. He was on shore and wagging his tail when the rescuers arrived!

28. Out With The Old, In With The New!

Frequently Asked Question

We're planning a wilderness canoe trip and want to be prepared with the best equipment. I hear there's a great new trail stove (tent, rain coat, canoe pack, etc. etc.) on the market which is absolutely terrific. It was top rated in the last issue of *Fun Canoeing Magazine*. What do you think of this new stove? Should I buy one?

Hightech Harry

The Answer

Dear Hightech:

Don't take magazine product tests too seriously. Writers work on deadline and are usually paid by the length of copy they produce not the time they spend researching and field-testing. Time is money, so research and product testing are kept to a minimum. Bad reviews mean losing advertisers, which are a magazine's life blood. For this reason, writers often tone down criticisms.

For example, many good tents have zippers which are too small. In the rugged world of the real outdoors, these zippers will fail—probably in the midst of a storm. But you'd better not write it that way. Ever notice how often the word may appears in equipment evaluations?

Frankly, the term expedition proven doesn't mean much any more. Most modern canoe expeditions don't last long enough to prove anything. I once made a three week canoe trip where it didn't rain at all. Needless to say, my rain gear worked perfectly!

The best advice I can give you when choosing equipment is to carefully examine everything before you buy. If a zipper looks weak, it probably is. If there's a plastic knob that can burn off or break, it likely will. How will the product perform in high winds or when it's caked with mud or soaked with rain? Will it break if you drop it? Can you repair it in the field without special tools?

Be aware that some of the most highly touted products which work flawlessly over the short haul, fail miserably when the weeks turn to years. So be wary of advertising claims and the testimonials of individuals whose experience is limited to a few trips. Instead, seek the advice of those who travel wild places year after year. These are the real experts, even though their opinions are seldom seen in print.

All this can be summarized in a single word—trust! Why change, If your old tent, trail stove or rain gear has never let you down? On the other hand, if your old stuff is worn out, or you suspect something better has come along, try the new item for a time—a long time, before you commit to it for an expedition. Trust doesn't come in two weeks!

In case you're wondering, my personal trial period is two canoeing seasons, which for me, translates into about ten weeks of actual field use.

29. Helpful Advice?

Scenario

You are canoeing across Saganaga Lake in the Boundary Waters Canoe Area of Minnesota, heading towards the Northern Lights portage. A cold, chilling rain has been falling steadily for hours. Thank goodness you have good rain gear and are wearing wool and polypropylene.

As you round the point, you come upon a group of teenagers who are stroking along in dead silence. "How's it goin'?" you call encouragingly. Groans of displeasure follow. You come alongside the lead canoe and exchange pleasantries with the adult leader. A teenage girl, wearing a poncho, sits shivering in the cold, wet bottom of the aluminum canoe. Her lips are blue and her skin is chalky white. In the bow, is another girl of similar age: she's not smiling but she looks okay.

The Question

This looks like a serious case of hypothermia in the making. Should you say something to the adult leader or smile and paddle on? Is this girl in real trouble, or is she simply cold? The leader looks none too happy—your advice may backfire and he may give you an earful of his own. Suppose he brushes you off and continues down the lake?

Should you mind this other leader's business or stick to your own?

Action Taken

I was the passing canoeist and had my own group of teenagers in tow. But they were all dressed appropriately and were singing or smiling. I was annoyed that the kids in the other group were hurting and the responsible adult either didn't know or care. So I firmly grabbed the bull by both horns and declared: "I think you guys better stop and warm up—that young lady in the middle isn't doing too good."

"How ya doin', Linda?" asked the leader.

"I'm okay," she whimpered softly.

Linda was not okay, so I pressed the issue with serious talk about hypothermia.

There was another round of "I'm okay, I'm okay," from the girl—and a "Can ya hang on till we stop for lunch?" From the leader. Hearing this, I cut across the lead canoe and with a great big smile said,

"C'mon, you guys, let's put ashore on that point." Strangely, everyone followed suit without argument.

The leader became deeply concerned when he saw that Linda could not get out of the canoe without help from friends. Then, everyone pitched in to set up a tent, make fire and re-warm the girl. The leader and I parted as friends, and the youngsters in both groups made new friends.

The Answer: Best Possible Course Of Action

This experience took place in 1980 when hypothermia was a hot new topic. The adult in Linda's canoe was concerned about her welfare; he just didn't think the situation was serious. He reasoned she was cold, that's all. But so was everyone else. Frankly, I was reluctant to butt in: I had my own responsibilities and didn't need his. But, would Linda have been okay if I hadn't pressed the point?

You don't have to travel to the Boundary Waters or to the high Arctic to find a life-threatening situation. Witness the canoeists who don't have rain gear or a dry change of clothes—and who have life jackets but never wear them. Should you say something when you observe an unsafe situation? Yes! Should you press the issue? Absolutely! Loss of life is too high a price to pay for ignorance or egotism.

Admittedly, your advice will not always be welcome, especially in the matter of life jackets and proper dress. One can only do what one can do. Fortunately, for those who will listen, it is sometimes enough.

30. Suited For The Wet

Frequently Asked Question

My friends and I will be making a three week canoe trip in the Northwest Territories next summer. The river we've selected has lots of big rapids! We've heard the water is very cold and that hypothermia is almost a sure thing in a capsize. Some of our whitewater friends have advised us to bring wet suits. Others suggest dry suits. Still others say that a sleeveless neoprene top or paddling shirt provides enough protection. What do you say?

Ron Rubatex and Bubba

The Answer

Dear Ron and Bubba:

This question comes up a lot and it's not an easy one to answer. Barren lands rivers vary in character as much as the ones in your home state.

You say your river has lots of rapids. Do you plan to run them all? If you're like most wilderness canoeists you'll canoe the obvious Class II-III stuff and line or portage around the rest. Running huge rapids in a tripping canoe sounds fearfully exciting. It is, especially the fearful part! Caution is the key word when you've got two thousand dollars worth of gear and food aboard and are three hundred miles from the nearest road. Even if you are very skilled, you won't take chances on an Arctic river!

My advice? Bring wet suits, dry suits or similar paraphernalia only If you'll be paddling long stretches of ice-cold Class III-IV rapids in a fully covered canoe or kayak. Otherwise, leave the sweaty paddling outfits at home. Here's why:

Most wilderness canoe trips—even those which may be rightfully categorized as white water—are seldom more than ten percent rapids. That's ninety miles of grueling flat water paddle work to ten miles of yee ha! And if the yee ha is questionable, you'll line or portage.

A typical day in the barrens looks like this:

The day begins with chilling drizzle and a light breeze, so you put on rain gear and snap down the splash cover. Two hours later, the sun comes out and the thermometer hits seventy. The wind stops dead and the black flies attack. Suddenly, you're sweating bullets. Off come the rain clothes and canoe cover. On go the DEET-impregnated bug jacket and head net.

Round the bend is a quarter mile long pitch which must be scouted. You tie up on shore and dutifully walk the rapid, making mental notes as you go. Thirty minutes and a buggy half mile later, you're back in the canoe again. You paddle one hundred yards, line the next twenty-five, then portage three hundred to the next bend, around which is a half mile of shallows. One minute you're paddling, the next you're wading, lining or dragging the canoe. Ultimately, you give up in disgust and portage the remaining quarter mile to the big lake below.

Add black flies and mosquitoes, plus a wet or dry suit and try this scene again. If the heat doesn't kill you, your own sweat will!

Why not put on paddling gear just before you enter a tough rapid, then take it off at the end? Sounds good, but it can be an awful hassle, especially when you're in the canoe and paddling one minute, and lining, portaging, wading or swatting bugs the next. Say, in the midst of all this you spot a herd of muskox on the hill a mile away and want to sneak up for a closer look. I'll bet you'll want to cast off the neoprene before you begin your walk.

I think you'll find that paddling suits—even breathable Gore-Tex® ones—are too hard to get on and off, and too hot and confining to wear for long periods. They are also bulky to pack—and pack space is at a premium on a long canoe trip.

There are exceptions, of course. You may want to struggle with special paddling gear if you'll be canoeing long sections of technical rapids just after snow melt. However, long, tough rapids are really the realm of kayaks and slalom canoes, not Canadian open canoes—even ones that are equip-ped with splash covers.

Some wilderness canoeists compromise by donning a light Gore-Tex® paddling shirt just before they enter big rapids. Others, including some of the best known names in the sport—Bob Dannert, Fred Gaskin, Alan Kesselheim and Mary Pat Zitzer, George Luste, Verlen Kruger, Steve Landick, Bob Ohara, Bill Simpson and Michael Peake—don't wear wet or dry suits on barren lands canoe trips. They rely instead on polyester, wool and waterproof nylon, topped with common sense and caution. I suggest you try the same recipe.

31. The Skills Of Your Partner

BRACE! BRACE!

Scenario

You're canoeing the lower stretch of the Steel River in northern Ontario. Rapids range from riffles through Class II. There's one short pitch which rates Class III, but it's easily runnable if you know how to brace and turn. You've canoed the Steel three times before and know every rock and eddy.

You're paddling a sixteen and one-half foot Kevlar Mad River explorer, which is ideal for the rugged twisting drops on the lower Steel. You're an instructor level white water canoeist; your bow partner—a woman in her late thirties—has never canoed in rapids.

It is the fourth day of your canoe trip and you and your partner are getting along great. She learns fast, has good balance and is eager to please. She flawlessly performs the basic turning strokes at your command. Call out, "draw!" And the bow turns left: yell, "cross-draw!" And it goes right. You are an impressive team; it's hard to believe this woman is a beginner. You trust her more and more with every mile you paddle and every small rapid you run. She's earns A+ in every maneuver—as long as you tell her what to do. So far, you've run every drop you've come to, and without a hint of tipping over.

Finally, the dreaded Class III rapid looms ahead and you pull into an eddy to discuss your plans. "You wanna run or portage?" You ask.

"I dunno," she says, "Whatever you think."

"Okay, we gotta go right of that rock," pointing, "into the vee below. Then, it's a quick left and we're home free. Got it?"

"I think so."

"Don't worry; I call right or left when it's time!"

The Question

Would you run this rapid or portage around it? Clue: re-read the scenario, specifically the conversation, and see if you can find a flaw. There's a big one and it's not obvious!

Action Taken

They decided to canoe the rapid. Coming through the vee, the man yelled left! The woman (who was paddling on the left) executed a crossdraw which pulled the bow right. Left! The man screamed again, and the woman did another cross-bow draw. Seconds later, the canoe crashed the rock and capsized. The crunching sound they heard was the Kevlar breaking up!

The Answer: What Went Wrong

The man had trained the woman with the terms draw and crossdraw. But when the crisis appeared, he yelled left! Moot point? Hardly. Well-trained beginners will do what you tell them, but they won't respond to commands they haven't learned. Certainly, the woman knew which way was left. She just didn't know which stroke to use to turn the canoe that way!

It takes a long time to develop reliable river running skills. Beginners lack the background—the feel of the river—that comes from a practiced understanding of canoes and currents. Have you ever noticed how quickly teenagers learn? And how fast they forget? Trained beginners have the earmarks of experts—that is, as long as their captains tell them what to do.

It takes two competent paddlers to run complex whitewater, especially when the way ahead requires rapid decisions. Mastering a new paddle stroke is easy; knowing when and where to use it, must be slowly simmered in a brew of practice and time. Remember this, before you try a tough maneuver with a partner who lacks your experience.

32. Mad About Bugs

Frequently Asked Question

I'm going to the Boundary Waters for the first time this summer and have heard they have giant mosquitoes that will eat you alive. Friends who've been there, also say I should watch out for black flies, giant bulldog flies and tiny critters called no-see-ums. Good grief! The BWCA doesn't sound like a very friendly place. Naturally, I plan to bring plenty of bug dope, but I'm concerned that this may not be enough to discourage the hungry critters. I've read that the best repellents contain a chemical called DEET, which isn't very good for your health. Is there anything, besides repellents, that will keep these bugs at bay?

Neurotic Innevada

The Answer

Dear Neurotic:

Your best hope is bug dope. As you indicate, the most effective repellents contain DEET—a chemical that contains N,N-diethyl-m-toluamide. Generally, the more DEET a repellent has, the better it works. However, too much DEET may be harmful to you! Very strong repellents may burn sensitive skin and dissolve the plastic frames of your eye glasses. They may even melt your polypropylene long underwear!

No one knows for sure how much DEET you need to keep bugs away. Everyone's body chemistry is different. However, experience in the Canadian Arctic suggests that 25 percent DEET, in a mixture with other ingredients, is enough for the meanest bugs—like black flies! The remainder of the repellent should be a soothing lotion or alcohol. Lotion is kinder to your skin and it evaporates slower than alcohol, which means the repellent lasts longer. You'll know it's time to rub in more repellent when the bugs start biting you again!

Build A Skin-Barrier With Sun Block

Kurt Avery, President of Sawyer Products, Inc. suggests you rub sun block deep into your skin, wait ten minutes, then apply the repellent. The sun block keeps your body from absorbing too much of the repellent. If possible, select one of the new bonding base sun blocks which penetrate deep into your skin. Film base sun blocks cover just the surface of your skin.

Head nets provide another tier of protection. A head net that doesn't have a hoop around the face is best because it rolls to fist size and fits in your pocket. Head nets cost only a few dollars at camping shops. Or, sew your own from bulk mosquito netting. Tip: it's much easier to see through black netting than tan or olive drab. Some bug-eyed paddlers use a black magic marker to darken the eye panel of their head net. Bring two head nets on every canoe trip, just in case you misplace or lose one.

Bug jackets are a God-send. They're breathable cotton-mesh jackets which you treat with nearly pure DEET to keep bugs from biting through. You must wear a long-sleeved shirt underneath to keep the caustic DEET away from your skin. The DEET treatment usually lasts about a week.

Some other types of bug jackets are made from stiff netting that hangs away from your body. Others resemble closely woven cotton windbreakers. I prefer the DEET-treated mesh, which lets breezes in and sweat out. You'll find many types of bug jackets at bait and tackle shops. Prices start around $25.

Make A Susie BugNet

The Susie BugNet was designed by my wife, Sue Harings, who is an avid wilderness explorer. It provides a bug-free environment for eating, sitting around the campfire, sleeping under the stars and when nature calls. Two or more people can fit inside. The net weighs almost nothing and it doesn't take up much space. It doubles as a luxurious pillow or light blanket.

To make a Susie BugNet, you'll need a piece of mosquito netting 60-72 inches wide and eight feet long, plus enough cord to go around the hem. Don't use no-see-um net; it's not strong enough and you can't see through it.

Fold the netting lengthwise to make a rectangular sheet which measures about eight feet by six feet. Sew up the long sides and hem the bottom. Install a tie cord in the hem and you're done. Commercial Susie BugNets are available from Cooke Custom Sewing (see Short F.A.Q.'s, #1)

Know Your Enemies!

Mosquitoes

Mosquitoes like to bite at dawn and dusk, and just before an approaching storm. They're mild-mannered compared to flies. The most gentle repellents will keep them away.

Horse flies, Deer flies and Bulldogs

Horse flies and Deer flies are much larger than House flies. They're most active at mid-day, when the sun is up. They zoom in like fighter planes (they prefer bare ankles) and produce painful wounds that may become infected if you don't clean them quick. Fortunately, they can't bite through socks or clothing. Bulldogs are the largest and meanest flies you'll find in Minnesota and Canada. However, they're slow moving and easy to kill. Thick wool socks stop them cold.

Tip: Benadryl® is excellent medication for insect bites.

Black Flies

Black flies, which are about the size of a rice grain, are the most dreaded pests in the north country. They happily swim in the strongest repellents, then they get up and fly away! Head nets and tightly woven clothing are your best defense.

Black flies breed in the fast water of rivers and are most prevalent around rapids and falls—so be wary where you camp. If you see their breeding socks—which resemble black nylon hose—on rocks in rapids, skeedaddle fast!

Black flies have tiny mouths, so you may not feel their bite. But, they leave a bloody wound which may swell as large as a golf ball!

Biting Midges (No-see-ums)

They're called no-see-ums because they are so tiny they can fly right through the holes in mosquito netting! Their bite feels like the jab of a hot needle. The pain goes away fast but the wound itches for some time. You can get special no-see-um netting, but its tiny holes make it hard to see through and hot to wear. Any good repellent will keep no-see-ums at bay.

The Answer

Outsmart Bugs With These Tricks!

1. Avoid navy blue clothes. Mosquitoes love this color! Generally, light colors are better than dark ones.
2. Bugs will stay away from your face if you saturate a handkerchief with repellent and tie it loosely around your neck. Spray the underside of your hat brim too!
3. Tuck your pant legs into high socks. Secure rubber bands over the socks. Also, rubber-band the wrists of your long-sleeve shirt, or use Velcro® bands on the openings.
4. Bugs can't bite through long underwear. Wear a thin suit under your clothes, if it's not too hot.

33. Weathered In

Scenario

Everyone who has canoed the Hood River in the Northwest Territories of Canada, speaks almost religiously of their encounter with Wilberforce Falls. Highest falls north of the Arctic Circle, and third highest in North America, Wilberforce drops 160 feet straight down, then, with an awesome pounding that can be heard for miles, it cuts its way through a two-mile red-rock canyon, spewing man-sized waves all the way. The three-and-one-half mile portage around Wilberforce is a grueling all-day affair. If, like most canoeists, you begin your trip at the headwaters of the Hood, you'll need about two weeks to reach the falls. Once you get there, you'll want to spend some serious time there. Sure, you can see Wilberforce Falls in a day, but if your schedule permits, you'll take three or four.

In 1982, a team of Americans set out to canoe the Hood River. They began at Point Lake, 200 miles south of the Hood, or 400 miles from its mouth at Bathurst Inlet. The crew planned to spend thirty-one days canoeing, three of them at Wilberforce Falls.

The weather turned sour three days before they were to arrive at Wilberforce Falls. Fifty to sixty mile per hour winds, accompanied by unusually heavy rains and temperatures in the thirties, kept the crew pinned down for sixty-two hours. There was nothing to do but sleep and pray the tents would hold.

On the morning of the third day of their isolation, the crew assembled for a monumentous decision. The wind had dropped to a measured ten miles per hour and the driving rain had turned to icy drizzle. The air temperature was 37°F and the river was in flood stage. The view downstream was darkened by silt and clogged with uprooted willows. Man-sized waves piled up on every outside bend and rapids mysteriously emerged from every break in the shoreline. What was, a few days ago, a benign and gentle flow, was now a raging torrent.

One of the crew members inserted a thermometer into the brown, muddy water of the Hood. The mercury slowly rose to 40 degrees!

The crew was sorely disappointed. They had planned to arrive at Wilberforce two days ago. If they left right now, they might make it by nightfall. That would allow a few hours down time at the falls. If they waited another day, they would see Wilberforce from under a canoe yoke as they walked the portage trail. Precious time—planned time— was slipping by. Wilberforce Falls was the highlight of their trip and now, except in passing, they might not see it at all.

The crew's leader, a tall energetic man in his mid-forties, was the accomplished veteran of two Arctic rivers—the Coppermine and Back. He was cautious and precise, and ordinarily reluctant to take chances. Nonetheless, Wilberforce was special: precious time was slipping by!

The leader cast a long knowing look towards the river and with deep concern said, "I think we better go now—we can't afford to sit here any longer." All five crew members—four of which were experienced leaders in their own right—objected.

"The river's too high, too fast, too dangerous. At least, let's wait till the rain stops—it's hypothermia city out there! Capsize and we're dead! Look at those waves, man; how'll we ever get down river?"

The leader listened then polled his crew. Except for him, no one was for going on.

There was a long cold silence, then the leader arose and grabbed his paddle. "We go!" he said. "Let's get moving. Now!"

The Question

Will you follow your leader or mutiny and wait for better weather? Consider the consequences of staying put. Remember, your leader is highly experienced, and he cares deeply about the welfare of his crew. The weather is improving some but it may be days before the sun comes out. And it may take another week before the river drops to what is normally considered a safe level for canoeing. Finally, be aware that time is running out. Your float plane will pick you up at the mouth of the river in three days. If you leave right now, you'll have a few hours to enjoy Wilberforce Falls—and you'll be where you're supposed to be when you're supposed to be!

On the other hand, there's no denying the dangers of the river. Current speed is at least ten miles an hour! If you capsize in the flow or miss a cross-stream ferry and plow into the big waves on an outside bend, you'll die for sure. What to do?

Action Taken

Despite considerable grumbling, the crew decided to follow their leader. The ten-mile paddle to Wilberforce Falls took nearly three hours. They took no chances, paddling within inches of the shoreline whenever possible and lining their canoes around questionable obstacles. Giant waves on the outside bends forced them to ferry to the inside curve every time the river changed directions. Later, the crew agreed that the frequent river crossings, which often carried them through waves of monster proportions, were the most dangerous experiences of their trip.

Would they do it again? Not a chance—even if it meant missing Wilberforce Falls and their float plane!

The Answer: With Due Respect

No one was hurt in this scenario, so it's tempting to suggest that the leader's decision was a good one. But the dangers were real—one miscalculation could mean disaster. Float plane be hanged—the crew should have waited for better weather!

It's interesting to note that all but the leader were against going on. No, none of the crew had ever paddled an Arctic river before, but all were skilled and experienced in their own right. Are four heads better than one? Not always. But given the experience of this crew and the obvious dangers of the river and the weather, the answer here is an unequivocal yes!

When bets are placed and shattered dreams loom just around the bend, there is a human side to all of us—even the most experienced and cautious—which must be addressed. It's when things get really hairy that the wisdom of many minds and conservative ways shine through.

I was on that Hood River canoe trip. I followed my leader when I should have followed my heart.

34. Les Mis-erables

I am indebted to Kevin Callan, Canadian canoeist, photographer and author, for this scenario which took place on a recent canoe trip in Algonquin Provincial Park. Kevin's latest book, *Up The Creek*, A Paddler's Guide to Ontario, The Boston Mills Press, 1996, details more reasonable Algonquin canoe routes than the one that is described here.

Scenario

Every year, you and some special friends make an annual pilgrimage to Algonquin Provincial Park in Ontario. This year, the group has decided to travel up the remote Raven Creek—which you will later discover is a forever twisting, narrow channel that's clogged with alder thickets and fallen trees. It's irritable work tunneling through the labyrinth—branches scraping against your itchy, bug-bitten body and showering you with dried leaves and spider webs. The physical irks, however, are minor compared to the confusion created by your attempts at maneuvering the seventeen-foot canoes around the constant twists and turns of the waterway.

It was the group's plan to navigate up the muddy stream and make it all the way to Erables Lake by the second day out. But, at 5:30 pm on day two, you're barely halfway! To make matters worse, your canoe partner and best friend, Scott, who has an amazing affinity to test the limit of his own endurance, tries to coax the rest of the group into continuing on.

The Question

This difficult route was chosen months before while your group nursed a keg of beer and shared stories and slides of previous outings. Halfway through the keg the group decided that next year's trip should be more challenging! On the map, Raven Creek looked simple, cutting somewhat of a clear path through the land. But now, things are much different. An informal poll reveals that everyone but Scott wants to turn back. Last winter, during the planning stages of this canoe trip, you reluctantly agreed to assume the role of group leader, even though you didn't want the job. Now, everyone is looking to you for answers. Going with the wishes of the group will hurt Scott's feelings. Suddenly, everything has become quite awkward.

Will you put on your leadership cap and make a decision? Or will you let Scott choose for the group? Scott is adamant about finishing what he started; you and your friends have had enough. Remember that everyone agreed to this trip last winter!

Action Taken

Scott's partner refused to accept command and the group dolefully continued on. Soon after, the creek narrowed to just a little wider than the width of the canoe, forcing the party to portage over an unmaintained trail to unspectacular Tillie Lake. They were just about to begin an 870 meter portage into yet another meandering, snake-like creek that eventually flows into Erables Lake, when the crew mutinied!

They then made camp directly beside the take-out to the long portage. It was a disappointing spot, with just enough space for the three tents to crowd together on top of a cleared patch amongst a patchwork of scraggly spruce. In the fading light of a golden evening they all sat around a smoldering fire, sipping gin and cherry Kool-aid from enamel cups while Scott prepared dinner for the group—a fitting punishment for urging everyone on without a hint of diplomacy.

Up early the next morning, fueled by a breakfast of flapjacks and camp coffee—also prepared by Scott, the newly appointed camp cook—the paddlers hauled their gear over the portage and made their way down Maple Creek to Erables Lake—a grueling five hour trip that Scott had previously estimated as a two hour trek, at most!

The Answer: Most Probable Course Of Action

It's a common theme—one usually skilled and articulate individual, insensitively presses forth to realize his dream, knowing full well that others don't share it. The plan to continue on smacks of credibility—after all, everyone did agree to it last winter. And they knew the route wouldn't be easy!

It takes courage to abandon a bad decision, especially when the commitment has been made and the scenario has begun. That's why every group needs a leader who is willing to make decisions and is sensitive to the wishes of the group. A good leader assumes command in matters of safety, logistics and social concerns and whenever the group cannot reach an equitable decision. All other issues are best handled democratically, even if the outcome does not reflect the goals of the leader. Remember, we're all family on a canoe trip, and no fighting please!

There's a natural urgency and noble merit to go with the plan and to finish what was started. As this case reveals, this is not always best. If the crew had to be at a certain place at a certain time, and going up the creek was the only way to get there, then Scott's way was the right way. However, at stake here, was a week of fun in a popular park. Saving face was the reason this crew chose to continue on. A heavy thread of martyrdom and animosity is woven into the story: the crew did it for Scott not for themselves. In the end, they rebelled at Scott's pushiness and punished him with kitchen duty.

When the perceived leader of this canoe trip failed to take command, Scott stepped in. Then, conditions deteriorated, largely because the group did not recognize Scott's authority. I'll bet that attitudes would have been less inflamed if their elected leader—not Scott—had made the unpopular decision to continue. The crew was well into the scenario when they realized their prediciament, so there was no guarantee that going back was easier than going on. What they needed most was a sensitive decision, even if it was not the one they wanted to hear. The leader might simply have said, "Well guys, we goofed: going on won't be easy, but it may be no harder than retracing old ground. There's adventure on the wind; I say we go on!"

Such an authoritatively sensitive decision would be respected by the group and, given the circumstances, probably considered reasonable. At most, an unfavorable outcome would be regarded as a group decision.

35. First, Be Sure You're Right!

Scenario

It's 1968 and you and a friend are making your first trip to the Boundary Waters Canoe Area of Minnesota. You are an Eagle Scout and have some basic first aid training. Your friend is a high school football coach who has treated scores of injuries on the playing field.

You are having lunch at the Hansen Lake portage (Gunflint Trail area) when a group of teenage boys and girls come on the scene. Two husky boys are carrying a girl of about fifteen on a stretcher. The girl is moaning and obviously in pain. Curious about her condition, you and your friend wander over and have a look.

"What's the problem?" Asks the Eagle Scout.

"Ah, she's got a bad stomach ache," comes the reply.

"How long she had it?

"Couple days."

"Have ya given her any medicine?" asks the football coach.

"Yeah, we been giving her Tums® and Exlax® (a laxative) but it doesn't seem to do much good."

The football coach presses his hand lightly on the right, lower quadrant of the girl's abdomen. She screams and he jerks his hand away. He asks the girl where she "first started hurting." She points to her belly button and says, "Here."

"Have you had any diarrhea?" He asks.

"No."

The Question

Is the girl in serious danger or is this a passing condition? Evacuating her will take the better part of a day. It's around a ten-hour paddle from Hansen Lake to Trail's End Landing on Saganaga Lake—the crew's take out point. The Canadian Customs station at Cache Bay, is about four hours away. From there, a float plane could fly her to the hospital in Grand Marais, eighty miles to the south.

On the other hand, the group's two adult leaders don't seem too worried. They—and the girl—are convinced that her illness is due to some swamp water she drank a few days ago. The girl is certain that her condition isn't serious.

Here are your options:

1. Stay out of it—it's none of your business.

2. Advise the group to increase the dosage of the two medications.

3. Tell them not to give her any more medication.

4. Poignantly advise the group to evacuate the girl immediately! Build a smoky signal fire with hopes of attracting a Forest Service spotter plane. Decide whether she should be taken to Canada Customs or Trail's End Landing.

Action Taken

The coach diagnosed the problem as acute appendicitis. He was particularly concerned about the laxative, which may already have caused serious infection. He strongly suggested that they evacuate the girl immediately to the Ranger station at Cache Bay.

"Empty a canoe and have your two strongest paddlers take her to Cache Bay," suggested the Eagle Scout. "The rest of the crew will follow as fast as they can. John and I will stay here and build a signal fire. Hopefully, we can attract a Forest Service field crew or float plane."

The leaders reluctantly agreed to this procedure.

Then, a miracle. As they were loading the girl into the canoe, a Forest Service float plane flew overhead. The Eagle Scout flashed the mirror of his Silva Ranger compass at the plane. A flash caught the pilot's eye.

Meanwhile, the coach put the kids in a long line and directed them to do "jumping jacks." Why jumping jacks? "I dunno; figured it was better than waving," he later said.

The plane dropped a wing and swooped in for a closer look; then landed on the lake. The pilot was hopping mad: "Better have a good reason to bring us down," he admonished! Then, he looked at the girl, and knew. The men carefully loaded the girl into the Cessna and prayed she'd be okay.

When the football coach and Eagle Scout finished their trip a week later, they stopped at the Forest Service headquarters in Grand Marais to inquire about the girl. Sure enough, it was appendicitis. Her condition, which had been aggravated by the laxative, was very serious. The Cessna landed on the beach at Grand Marais and the girl was taken to the hospital. Her appendix was removed within the hour.

"Thanks to you guys, she's okay," grinned the Ranger.

The hero in this story is John Orr, a senior social studies teacher from Indianapolis, Indiana. I was the Eagle Scout.

The Answer: Most Probable Course Of Action

John and I knew that evacuating the girl would spoil everyone's canoe trip, so we were reluctant to suggest it. But John was emphatic: he was certain it was appendicitis. John's quick thinking—and refusal to give in to the "I'm okay, I'm okay" ramblings of the girl—saved her life. That we, and a float plane just happened to be in the right spot at the right time, suggests that a greater power than ours was also on the scene.

Of course, John could have been wrong in this situation, and that would have been very embarrassing. But his confident diagnosis and cool persistence saved the day.

Daniel Boone got it right when he said, "First be sure you're right, then go ahead." That's good advice to follow on any canoe trip.

36. Pigs On A Picnic?

Scenario

You and your friend are kayaking a stretch of Lake Superior's north shore, near Minnesota's Gooseberry Falls State Park. It's eighty degrees and the lake is mirror calm. You stop for lunch at a government picnic site on a long, rocky point. It hasn't rained for weeks and the woods are tinder dry. You're not surprised to see newly erected signs that read **DANGER: DRY CONDITIONS—NO CAMPFIRES ALLOWED**. No problem; lunch is easy— bagels and cream cheese, candy bar and orange drink— and you're on your way. No need for a fire, even if it were allowed.

About fifty yards away a young family is enjoying a picnic at another site. They are roasting weiners over a huge bonfire. A little boy, about six is playing by the water's edge. He has a plastic bucket filled with beer and pop cans and is tossing the cans into the lake. His parents seem oblivious to what he's doing.

The Question

The family is in violation of the law on at least two accounts—making fire where it's not permitted, and polluting a public lake. Should you say you don't approve? Report them to authorities? Or, mind your own business and continue your trip? Suppose the man becomes hostile and spoils everyone's good time? This is the United States of America; it is a public facility, remember?

Action Taken

The kayakers approached the family with a glowing smile and remarked, "I'm sorry to interrupt your picnic, but did you guys see the 'no campfires' sign?" The boy's father smiled at the intruders and said "It's no big deal; we'll put it out when we leave."

One of the kayakers then told the man that his son was throwing cans into the lake. The dad replied: "No way! Billie wouldn't do that. There's been 'stuff' floating by all day."

As the kayakers turn to go, they observe a huge pile of cans and bottles by the campfire. Then, with strained hostility, the kayakers return to their boats and finish their lunch. Shortly thereafter, the family prepares to leave. In minutes the fire is out and they are on their way to their car, which is parked about fifty yards away.

The boaters walk to the fire site and observe thick smoke still rising from the ashes. The fire grate is packed with tin cans, bottles and nylon cord. The men are hopping mad.

One of the boaters puts out the fire while the other runs to the man's car, which is about to take off for parts unknown. The windows of the car are closed and the air conditioner is running. The boater knocks on the window and it comes sliding down.

"Get out of the car and put out your fire, you pigs," says the kayaker.

"We didn't leave that stuff," says the man, in a genuinely embarrassed tone. "It was there when we got here!"

"Hardly," says the kayaker, with a look that could kill. As the car speeds merrily away he yells out, "We'll clean up your mess for you, you stinking pigs!" Then, he copies down the license plate and does what he promised. Later, he reports the incident to authorities.

The Answer: Most Probable Course Of Action

I think the kayakers did the right thing. They had a right to be angry, though they probably shouldn't have called the family pigs, even though they were. First, they tried the honey approach, "Hey, you guys, it says no campfires!" Then, they politely tried to tell the man and his wife that their son was trashing the lake. No luck: these people were either callused polluters or incredibly stupid. The honey went untouched; It was time to bring in the big guns! The man had a wife and two little kids in tow, so it was doubtful he would become violent. He didn't. Thanks to the persistence of the kayakers, the man did get a phone call from authorities, though no charges were filed.

If there's a lesson here, it is that everyone who loves wild places and the magic of canoes has a heart-felt responsibility to protect the environment. There are simply not enough police to guard the ranks of those who do not care. We must become involved, even when it means being politely assertive and sticking up for what we know is right.

SHORT F.A.Q.'S

15 of the most frequently asked canoeing questions:

1. **Where can I get a fabric splash cover for my canoe?**

    From: Cooke Custom Sewing, 7290 Stagecoach Trail, Lino Lakes, MN 55014-1988, (612) 784-8777 fax 784-4158

    Choose Cliff Jacobson's *three-piece* cover with expandable belly, or Bob O'Hara's three-piece style with split center-section. For solo canoes, there is the Jacobson two-piece style, and a three-piece model of Cooke's design. Dan Cooke will modify or custom build any canoe cover. Cooke Custom Sewing also makes great canoe packs, thwart bags and tarps—including the fully bug-netted *Tundra Tarp*, which Dan Cooke and I designed. Newest addition to the Cooke line is the practical **Susie BugNet**, which my wife, Sue Harings, designed.

2. **Where can I get old fashioned Duluth packs?**

    From: Duluth Tent & Awning Co., 1610 W. Superior St., Duluth, MN 55816-0024, 1-800-777-4439; and CLG Enterprises/Superior Packs, 3838 Dight Ave. south. Minneapolis, MN 55406, Phone: 1-800-328-5215

3. **My canoe has wood trim. Should I varnish or oil the trim?**

    Varnish is more durable than oil but the finish is harder to maintain. And, many canoeists dislike the plastic look of varnished wood. Old time marine spar varnish is trickier to apply than modern polyurethane's, but it's tougher. Oil maintains the flexibility of wood better than varnishes—which means that gunnels are less likely to break if the canoe wraps up. My favorite finishing oil is Djeks Olay®. Dagger Canoe Company agrees.

4. **My canoe has caned seats. What should I use to keep the cane soft and flexible?**

Cane is a natural material. It must *breathe* or it will become brittle and crack. Don't varnish caned seats. Varnish will cause the cane to dry out. Occasional applications of Djeks Olay®, Watco® or boiled linseed oil will keep your cane seats looking like new.

5. **Is it okay to store my canoe outside?**

Aluminum canoes can be stored in blazing sun, rain and snow, without problems. Plastic (fiberglass/Kevlar, Royalex, polyethylene) canoes deteriorate in the presence of ultra-violet light and should be protected from the elements. Don't ever cover a canoe with plastic sheeting! The color will fade and the plastic may deteriorate. Specialized outdoor covers—like those used on cars—are fine. Always store your canoe upside down, on saw horses, and in the shade. Never store a canoe on a concrete floor or near a garage window, where the sun can shine on it.

If you must store a plastic canoe outside and don't have a water-proof/breathable cover, apply a liquid ultraviolet inhibitor to the hull twice a year. Any hardware store can recommend suitable products.

Wooden canoes and wood-trimmed canoes cannot be left out in sun and rain for long periods of time.

6. **Where can I get adjustable portage pads that will fit on the carrying yoke of my canoe?**

From: Empire Canvas Works, PO Box 17, Solon Springs, WI 54873, 715-378-4216

7. **I want to drill holes for lining ropes in the ends of my canoe. How do I do this without wrecking my canoe?**

This method gives good results:

1. Mark a point half way down the stem of the canoe and 1.5 inches in.

2. Cut a 6" x 1" strip of paper and fold the paper around the stem of the canoe so one end intersects the marked point of the lining hole. Mark the hole location on the paper strip.

3. Remove the paper strip and fold it in half. Punch a hole through the folded paper at the marked point. Essentially, the paper strip is a template, like that used for installing door knobs and key holes.

4. Tape the paper around the nose of your canoe and use a one-eighth inch bit to drill through the hull from each side.

5. Remove the paper template and enlarge the hole from each side with a three-eighths inch diameter drill.

6. Use a rat-tail file to enlarge the hole to accept a one-half inch diameter length of PVC water pipe.

7. Glue (instant epoxy) the PVC pipe in the hole. Cut off the ends and smooth them with a file and pipe reamer. Then, spray paint the fitting to match the color of the hull.

8. **I feel like the seats in my canoe are too low. Is it safe to raise them?**

High seats make a canoe feel tippy; low ones add stability. Generally, high seats are more comfortable than low ones. And they allow a more relaxed and powerful stroke, especially if the canoe has deep sides.

If you don't like the height of your seats, change them—an inch at a time—until you are satisfied. Note: the more experience you gain, the higher you'll probably want to sit. Be sure to add one inch to the length of your canoe paddle for every inch you raise your seat!

9. **I have a lead on a good used Kevlar canoe. The canoe was damaged in a rapid and was carefully patched. The patch looks good (it's hardly noticeable). The salesman says the canoe "is as strong as new." Is he putting me on?**

No. A well-patched canoe is as strong as new—maybe stronger, depending on the materials and resin system used for patching. If you can find a good deal on a *well patched* canoe, buy it!

10. **Where can I get modern packs which are designed expressly for canoeing?**

Soft packs are available from:
JOHNSON CAMPING, INC., Camp Trails Division, 625 Conklin Rd., Binghamton, NY 13902, 800-847-1460
GRADE VI, Inc., POB 8, Urbana, IL 61801-0008
GRANITE GEAR, Inc., PO Box 278, Two Harbors, MN 55616, 218-834-6157
COOKE CUSTOM SEWING (See question #1)

Wanigans or dry boxes are available from:
YORK PACK, INC., 15 W. Main St., Yarmouth, ME 04096, 800-348-4923
STORMY BAY (formerly, "E.M. Wanigan"), Dennis Herdegen, PO Box 345, Grand Rapids, MN 55744, 218-326-5104

11. Some experts recommend that gear be tied into a canoe when running whitewater. Others say not to tie anything in. Who's right?

It depends. If rapids are short and have a *rescue pool* at the bottom, it may be best not to tie anything in. Long rapids—and those followed by miles of determined current—require some sort of *accountability* for gear, especially, if there are no *rescue boats* to pick things up.

I follow these rules:

1. I usually tie in gear when descending long, complex rapids. I secure everything so tightly that it can't float out and be caught in strainers or between rocks. Gear that floats out may cause a canoe to broach and wrap—a dangerous situation. For this reason, I never buckle pack straps to thwarts.

2. I don't tie in gear when rapids are short and have a rescue pool at the bottom, or when my fabric splash cover is snapped on the canoe. A splash cover usually stays with a capsized canoe and keeps gear from floating out.

12. My canoe has just one thwart in the center. Is this strong enough?

Not really. Canoes are flexible craft; hulls will eventually distort if they don't have cross-members to hold them in shape. Each thwart adds around two pounds to the weight of a canoe. Eliminate two of them and you've cut four pounds, which is pretty significant. Working canoes should have at least three thwarts—one behind the bow seat, one in the middle, and one about two feet forward of the stern seat. Wilderness and whitewater canoes should also have a short thwart just behind the bow and stern decks. Thwarts are the skeleton of your canoe—more bones make a stronger body! Every canoe shop has pre-cut ash thwarts. It takes only a few minutes to cut them to size and bolt them in.

13. **Some canoes are asymmetric—that is, the bow and stern don't have the same shape. Others are symmetrical. Is there an advantage in asymmetry?**

Yes and no. The widest point of an asymmetric canoe is usually a few inches to a foot behind center. This produces a narrow bow and a fat, buoyant stern. The thin bow presents a narrow wedge to the water, which makes for an easier turn of speed. The buoyant stern rises above the canoe's turbulence (wake) when the canoe is paddled hard. The effects of asymmetry are most noticeable in shallow water, but are significant at all depths.

On the other hand, symmetrical canoes may be more predictable, especially in tricky currents and when they're paddled backwards. However, this criticism was more valid two decades ago when high performance hulls boasted bizarre asymmetry which could often be seen well above the water line. Today's asymmetric canoes are a gentler, more elegant breed. Frankly, *narrowing the bow and widening the stern* to improve performance is nothing new. The American Indians built very classy—and very fast!—asymmetric birch bark canoes centuries ago!

14. What's the best footwear for canoeing?

You could start a war with this one. There are lots of options, none of them are perfect. Here are the alternatives:

1.   Most popular, are low-cut sneakers with wool socks. Low cut is important as it enables you to kick the shoes off if your foot becomes trapped between rocks in a capsize, or while you're wading.

2.   When the water's cold, wear wet-suit socks inside over-size sneakers. Or, wear Gore-tex® socks.

3.   L.L. Bean boots are the traditional solution to dry feet on wilderness canoe trips. Be sure you order the genuine sheepskin insoles, which are cooler and more breathable than synthetics.

4.   Sixteen-inch high rubber boots ("Green Wellies") are the choice of barren lands paddlers and cold water wilderness trippers.

5.   Neoprene booties with felt soles are ideal for wading in cold water. Wet-suit socks, worn inside canvas shoes that have felt soles, are also good. Nothing sticks to wet rocks like felt!

6.   Sixteen-inch high Tingley® rubber overshoes worn over canvas sneakers. Inexpensive Tingley's are available at construction supply stores. They work well everywhere, from the barrens to the Boundary Waters.

River sandals are okay for sandy bottomed streams but not for rocky rivers where pebbles may get caught between your toes when you wade. Wear sandals in the *north country* and the bugs will chew up your feet! Sandals are best for rafters who seldom have to wade, line or portage. Canoeists are better served with *more protective* footwear.

Every canoeist should bring two kinds of footwear on a canoe trip. Three kinds are better!

15. **We're going to canoe a wilderness river and plan to rent canoes from a local outfitter. What questions should I ask the outfitter? What things should I bring from home?**

1. Are the canoes equipped with comfortable portage yokes? If not, be prepared to bring your own! Note: canoeists and outfitters often have different ideas of what constitutes *comfort*. Remember this before you commit to a portage yoke you haven't seen!

2. Do the canoes have glued-in knee pads? If not, bring your own, plus some Weldwood™ Contact Cement to glue them in.

3. Canoes used on whitewater or barren lands routes should come equipped with fabric splash covers.

4. Bring your own life jackets and paddles. You'll like them much better than those supplied by outfitters.

5. If you are renting packs, ask the outfitter if he or she provides two heavy-duty (4 to 6 mil thick) waterproof plastic liners for each pack. If not, bring your own.

6. Supply your own canoe sponge, plastic bailer and twenty-five foot lining ropes. Bring some shock-cord to secure coiled ropes and small items.

7. Bring an assortment of tools—crescent wrench, common box wrenches, flat-tip and Phillips screwdrivers, and pliers. A Leatherman® or Gerber Multipliers® is standard equipment on canoe trips. Tighten all the bolts on your rental canoe before you begin your trip!

8. Ask about safe storage of your vehicle. If a shuttle is needed, be prepared to pay extra for it.

Glossary of Terms

Bailer: A scoop (usually made from an empty bleach jug by cutting off the bottom) for bailing the canoe.

Bow: The front end of a canoe.

Broach: To turn suddenly into the wind, or at right angles to the current in a river.

Broadside: A canoe that is perpendicular to the current of the river, thus exposing its broad side to obstacles in the water.

Carry: To carry a canoe and gear overland, to safer water. Same as *portage*.

Draw: Bow and stern paddlers use this powerful stroke to turn the canoe or *draw* it side-ways.

Eddy: The calm water below a rock that's protruding in a river. Eddy currents run *opposite* to that of the river's flow, and are often strong enough to stop a canoe in its tracks and prevent it from going downstream. Whitewater canoeists use eddies as *safe resting places* from the stress of running rapids. You'll also encounter eddys on the slow-moving inside bends of rivers.

Eddy Turn: Canoeists and kayakers use the *eddy turn* to enter an eddy from the river's main flow. Paddlers must *brace* strongly with their paddles as the canoe crosses the *eddy line,* which marks the location of the opposing currents. Eddy turns are for skilled paddlers.

Ferry: Moving laterally across a current, like a ferry boat.

Flatwater: Water without rapids, such as a lake or slow-moving river.

Flotation: Any buoyant material in a canoe that keeps it afloat in a capsize.

Grab Loop: A loop of rope on the bow or stern of a canoe. Provides a convenient hand hold.

Gunnels (gunwales): The upper rails of the canoe.

Hole (souse hole): A hole results when water flows over a rock in a strong rapid. Essentially, a hole is a powerful eddy set on edge. Some holes, like those at the base of waterfalls and dams, are called *keepers* because they trap and hold any canoe (or human!) that gets into them. Holes are the realm of the whitewater rodeo crowd: flatwater and wilderness paddlers should avoid them!

Keel: A vertical metal, plastic or wooden strip that runs along the center of the canoe's bottom.

Ledge: Another name for a waterfalls.

Line: Rope used to tie up a canoe or pull it around obstacles in the water.

Lining: Working a canoe *downstream* around obstacles in the water with the aid of lines. *Tracking* is the opposite of lining—it's *upstream* work.

Portage: Same as *carry*.

River Right, River Left: River right is the right side of a river, as viewed downstream. *River left* is the opposite.

Rocker: An upward curve of the keel line of a canoe. Whitewater canoes have lots of rocker; flatwater canoes have very little.

Splash cover: A fitted cover designed to keep water out of a canoe. Splash covers are useful in rough rapids and big waves.

Stem: The extreme ends of a canoe—the rising, near vertical part.

Stern: The back end of a canoe.

Strainer: Any obstacle in the river which can trap and hold a canoe. Downed trees are dangerous *strainers* because their branches retain canoes and swimmers.

Thwart: A cross brace that runs from gunnel to gunnel. Thwarts give strength and rigidity to the hull.

Trim: The difference in the draft at the bow and stern of the canoe. *Level trim* means the canoe is riding dead level in the water.

Tumpline: A strap that is secured just above a person's forehead to help support a pack or canoe.

Vee: an identifiably *safe path* through rapids. The route between rocks is marked by an obvious *vee.*

Wanigan: A large waterproof gear box.

Whitewater: Foamy (air-filled), turbulent water. Same as rapids.

Wrap (wrap-up): When a canoe capsizes in a rapid and *wraps* around a rock.

International Rapid Rating Scale

Water Class & Characteristics

I.   *Easy*

Easy bends, small rapids and obstacles which are easy to avoid. River speed is less than hard back-paddling speed.

II.   *Medium*

Fairly frequent but unobstructed rapids with regular waves and low ledges. River speed occasionally exceeds hard back-paddling speed. Class II is about the limit of loaded open canoes.

III.   *Difficult*

Small falls, large, regular waves covering boat. Expert maneuvering required. Current speed usually less than fast forward-paddling speed. A fabric splash cover is almost essential if you're paddling a loaded open canoe.

IV.   *Very Difficult*

High powerful waves and difficult eddies. Abrupt bends and difficult broken water. Powerful and precise maneuvering is mandatory.

V.   *Exceedingly Difficult*

Fast, powerful eddies, violent currents, steep drops.

VI.   *Limit of Navigability*

Navigable only at select water conditions by teams of experts. Those who run Class VI possess a significant death wish!

Try These Other Books By
Cliff Jacobson

- Canoeist's Q&A *Scenarios for Serious Canoeists* — $9.95

- Boundary Waters Canoe Camping With Style — $11.95

- The Basic Essentials of Map & Compass 2nd Edition — $6.95

- The Basic Essentials of Solo Canoeing — $6.95

- Canoeing & Camping — $12.95

- Canoeing Wild Rivers; Expanded and Updated Edition — $24.95

- The Basic Essentials of Knots for the Outdoors — $6.95

- Campings Forgotten Skills — $11.95

- The Basic Essentials of Cooking in the Outdoors — $6.95

- Camping Secrets — $11.95

- Campsite Memories *True Tails From Wild Places* — $11.95

- The Basic Essentials of Camping — $6.95

- Canoeist's Little Book of Wisdom — $5.95

ICS BOOKS, Inc.

For a free catalog of all ICS BOOKS titles call toll free 1-800-541 7323

Visit ICS on the World Wide Web at:
http://www.icsbooks.com
SEND E-MAIL TO: adventure@icsbooks.com